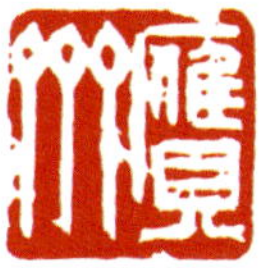

The stamp bears the Chinese characters 贗斋, ‘Fake Studio’

KETTLE'S YARD Ridinghouse

AI WEIWEI

THE LIBERTY OF DOUBT

EDITED BY ELIZABETH BROWN
& ANDREW NAIRNE

PREFACE

ANDREW NAIRNE &
ELIZABETH BROWN

> 'My name is Ai Weiwei. I am an artist, activist, writer and documentary maker. But first I am a human being.'

This precise and powerful declaration by Ai Weiwei is much more than a statement of fact. It is a manifesto that reflects a deep respect for the values that allow a full life. For those who have read Ai's memoir, *1000 Years of Joys and Sorrows* (2021), these words are all the more resonant in the context of his treatment in China, his survival and his subsequent exile from an authoritarian regime. As he recently said at an event in Cambridge: 'You have to stand up.' These values, especially freedom of expression, openness and the ability to use your talents, are fundamental to Ai's art and life. That his many and varied activities are inextricably connected to one another suggests an art not only of and about the world, but one determined to change it.

This new book accompanies the exhibition *Ai Weiwei: The Liberty of Doubt* at Kettle's Yard, a museum and gallery within the University of Cambridge. In his interview for this publication, the artist speaks about the exhibition title, noting that 'this ability and spirit to doubt have permeated the history of human thought and political struggle' and how 'the liberty of doubt' is 'a prerequisite for cultural and ideological development'. Yet under regimes around the world this liberty does not exist, while elsewhere it requires constant defence. Ai's consistent challenges to the Chinese state on its record of human rights abuses, including those of the Uighur population and the people of Hong Kong, continue to be censored.

In the exhibition, Ai Weiwei has juxtaposed historic Chinese objects with his own works for the first time. The antiquities were acquired by the artist at an auction in Cambridge in 2020. He has identified some as original, including from the Northern Wei dynasty (386–534 CE), and others as 'fakes', later copies, though this is a matter of judgement. As he notes, however, in China there is a long tradition of fluid, less fixed views in relation to authenticity, in an artistic culture that often values the act of copying. In his essay included here, James J. Lally explores this tradition further. Meanwhile, John Tancock notes in his essay considering the themes of the exhibition that these antiquities 'in exile' are perhaps an allegory for human migration and displacement, echoing the artist's own experiences.

In the same gallery as the antiquities is a version of *Dropping a Han Dynasty Urn*, one of Ai Weiwei's most famous works. Here the three original photographic frames have been reconstructed in a favourite material of the artist: LEGO. In the third of the three large-scale images, the artist looks outwards at us, the broken shards of the pot on the ground at his feet. His purposeful stare and the position of his raised hands echo the gesticulations of saints to be found in Renaissance painting. In contrast, the small Buddhist statues carved in stone nearby are in meditative poses designed to encourage belief in the viewer that spiritual enlightenment is the true path to change. Ai's iconoclastic act has come to be perceived as drawing attention to the Chinese leadership's wilful destruction of the country's heritage.

Ai Weiwei's own works in the smaller gallery, handmade to an exceptional standard in jade, marble and porcelain by Chinese artisans, explore contemporary issues, draw on his life story and transform familiar artefacts into iconic objects. Many of these sculptures act as microcosms of continuing social, political and cultural issues, such as handcuffs crafted in jade and a marble surveillance camera. Also included in the exhibition are three of the artist's recent documentaries. These remarkable films examine and illuminate the early days of the Covid-19 pandemic in Wuhan, the student protests in Hong Kong and the global crisis of forced migration.

In presenting compelling objects and images, Ai Weiwei reflects upon the liberty we have to express doubt and challenge authority – freedoms crucial for the vitality of culture and to achieve political and social change. Across the exhibition, which also encompasses Ai's love of cats and two of his *Fairytale Chairs* placed either side of a Henry Moore sculpture in the Kettle's Yard House, there is a tremendous breadth of ideas. As we encounter his highly material art, there is a sense that you need to get up close to be able to then step back. This ambitious, hugely imaginative, questioning art is as generous as it is profound. It is an exhibition, or, more, an encounter, the artist seems to say, that belongs not to him but to us.

In making the exhibition and this publication, we are enormously grateful to Ai Weiwei's studio team in Berlin, especially Jennifer Ng, Yun-hua Chen, Kimberly Sung, Gui Nuo and Xu Ye, and for the assistance of Wang Fen in Cambridge. The support of Lisson Gallery has been invaluable, and we are especially grateful to Greg Hilty and Courtney Plummer. Thank you to Dr James Lin for his invaluable support at the beginning of this project. The team at A Practice for Everyday Life have been tireless in their work to create a beautiful exhibition design and publication; thanks in particular go to Kirsty Carter, Daniel Griffiths and Matt Kay. We are thankful to Sophie Kullmann and Aimee Selby at Ridinghouse for their support in bringing the publication to life and ensuring its distribution. We are grateful to Thierry Bal for his remarkable portrait of Ai Weiwei, to Jo Underhill for her photographs documenting the exhibition, and to Tip Photo for their photographs of the Chinese 'real' and 'fake' objects. We are indebted to Dr Hajni Elias, who generously shared her expertise in relation to Chinese antiquities both for our public interpretation and within this catalogue; to James J. Lally for his prescient insights on the 'real' and 'fake'; and to John Tancock for his rich and expansive essay on Ai Weiwei and the importance of the liberty of doubt.

Huge thanks go to our supporters, without whom none of this would be possible: our Exhibition Circle, Patrons, Corporate Supporters, the Friends of Kettle's Yard and Arts Council England. As one of the eight University of Cambridge Museums, we benefit from and are embedded within a remarkable place of research, learning, insight and inquiry. This exhibition and book exemplify the values of the University of Cambridge and its mission to contribute to society.

We are grateful to our colleagues at Kettle's Yard, who have all played a part in making the exhibition, book and accompanying events happen. Our thanks go to Guy Haywood, Assistant Curator, for his expert handling of the complexities of this ambitious project, and to Tom Noblett, Programme Technician, who has overseen the beautiful gallery installation with Steve Penney, Facilities Manager.

Finally, our thanks to Ai Weiwei for devising this remarkable exhibition and enabling us to share his powerful and urgent work at Kettle's Yard. It has been a privilege to bring the exhibition to fruition, led by his creative ingenuity.

THE LIBERTY OF DOUBT

JOHN TANCOCK

Visitors to the Ai Weiwei exhibition at Kettle's Yard may initially be puzzled as 14 Chinese sculptures and objects, predominantly Buddhist in subject with the exception of one representing Laozi, are prominently displayed along with Ai's own works. They all belong to Ai, who happened to hear about them coming up for sale at auction in Cambridge, where for personal reasons he had moved in 2018. As a collector of such material, and hearing good things about the collector whose estate was being sold in December 2020, Ai thought there would be no harm in placing low bids, but he was not going to chase after anything. The collector in question was C. Roger Moss OBE, a prominent international businessman, who formed the collection while he was living in Hong Kong between 1980 and 2003.

Like C. Roger Moss, Ai knows many curators and dealers in the field of Chinese art, to whom he sent images of his purchases. Not surprisingly, the authenticity of a certain number was questioned, one of the specialists noting that he knew who was making some of them. None of this was at all unusual or surprising, as collectors of Chinese sculpture in the twenty-first century could attest. Furthermore, notes in the auction catalogue stated that 'the dating of Chinese sculpture is notoriously difficult and all such references in this catalogue are based entirely upon style and should not be relied upon as a statement of fact.'

Unexpectedly, the fact that some of the sculptures Ai had purchased may not be authentic offered a wonderful opportunity for him to establish a dialogue between the 14 antiquities and a selection of his own works that are related in varying ways to different aspects of classical Chinese art. Unconventional as it is, Ai's exhibition at Kettle's Yard, *The Liberty of Doubt*, is fully in keeping with Jim Ede's belief that 'The role of art is to give food for thought, to act as a stimulant, to entice the onlooker to inspect things, people, emotions from a new point of view.'[1]

NEW PERSPECTIVES

New perspectives were precisely what Ai Weiwei acquired during the almost 12 years he was living in the United States, mostly in New York, between 1982 and 1993. Of equal importance for the development of his current status as a public albeit controversial figure were his growing awareness of the multiple ways in which art had been redefined, which he was able to absorb at first hand unlike his contemporaries who remained in China, and a deepening understanding of the concept of liberty, even if Ronald Reagan's 'shining city on a hill' where 'the walls had doors and the doors were open to anyone with the will and the heart to get here' did not apply then and even less now.[2]

The numerous photographs Ai took of demonstrations, confrontations between the police and activists, and aircraft just returned from the Persian Gulf in Washington, DC testify to his growing political awareness, even if as an illegal immigrant he was unable to do anything about it, no more than he was on 4 June 1989, the date of the fatal confrontation between thousands of students and the military on Tiananmen Square in Beijing, unmentionable in China ever since.

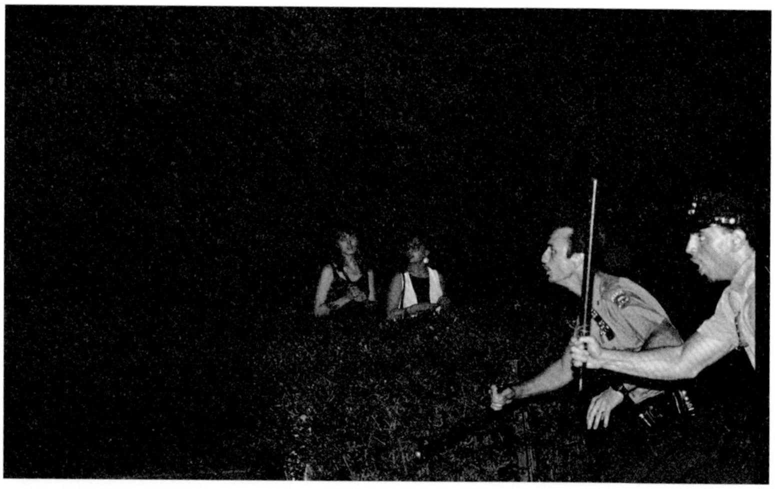

Ai Weiwei, *Tompkins Square Park Riot*, 1988

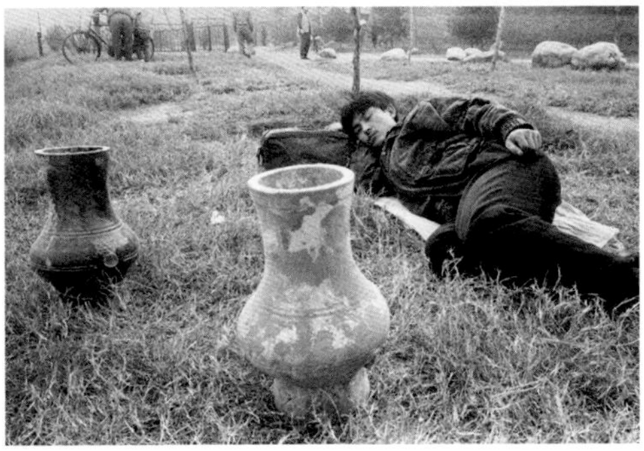

Ai Weiwei, *Antique Vendors, Xi'an*, 1993

After Ai's brief and not very successful period at Parsons School of Design in Greenwich Village, New York, he led a hand-to-mouth existence, as thousands of informal photographs he took reveal, socialised with the many Chinese artists, musicians and film-makers who started making pilgrimages to New York in the 1980s, and kept up with what was happening in the galleries, much of which was not to his liking. He did respond positively, however, to Andy Warhol (his writings as much as his paintings) and to Jasper Johns, through whose work he discovered Marcel Duchamp. He could conceivably have met Warhol but there was no overlap between Warhol's louche set with its propensity for night-clubbing and Ai's circle of Chinese strivers, and Johns was not at all accessible. It was through this artistic genealogy that Ai decided to abandon painting in about 1986 in favour of the making of objects, offspring of Duchamp's readymades.

REDISCOVERING BEIJING

Ai Weiwei returned to Beijing in 1993 to help take care of his father, the poet Ai Qing, whose health was beginning to decline. Back in the city of his birth and living in his family's traditional courtyard house close to the centre of the city, it was not 'the shock of the new'[3] that absorbed him but the familiarity with the old, the constant reminders of an ancient civilisation that were still readily accessible and underlie many aspects of modern life in China. Often in the company of his brother Ai Dan, who had extensive knowledge of Chinese classical art, he began frequenting the antiques markets that were a familiar feature not only in Beijing but elsewhere in China. Photographs taken in 1993 show a rowdy scene in Panjiayuan Antiques Market in Beijing and a sleeping vendor in Xi'an.[4]

As the economy heated up in China in the 1990s, aggressive modernisation led to the destruction of countless old buildings and entire neighbourhoods, a devastation that Ai was later to document

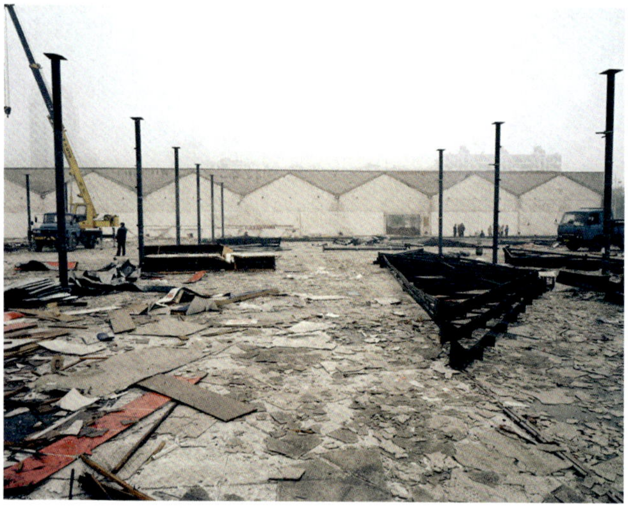
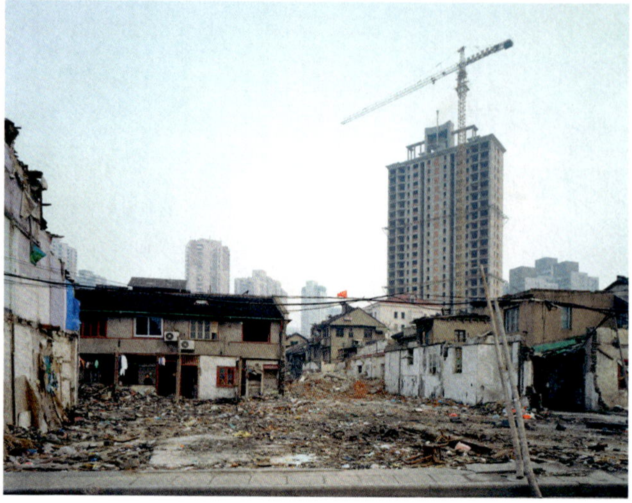
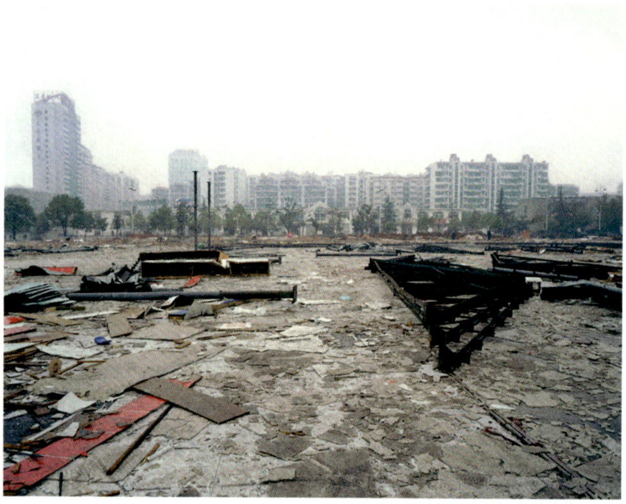
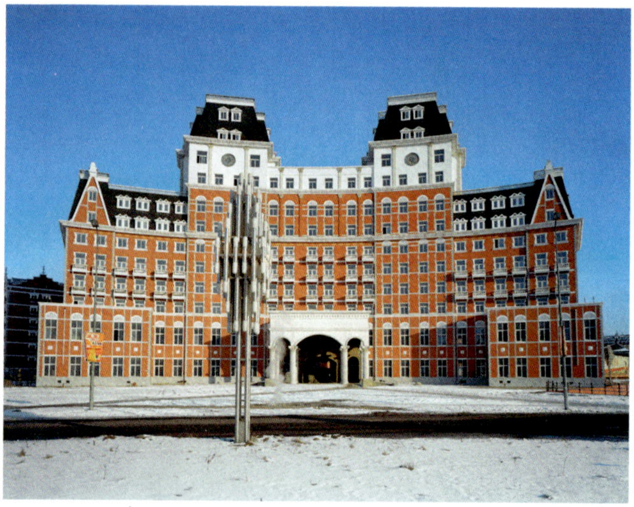
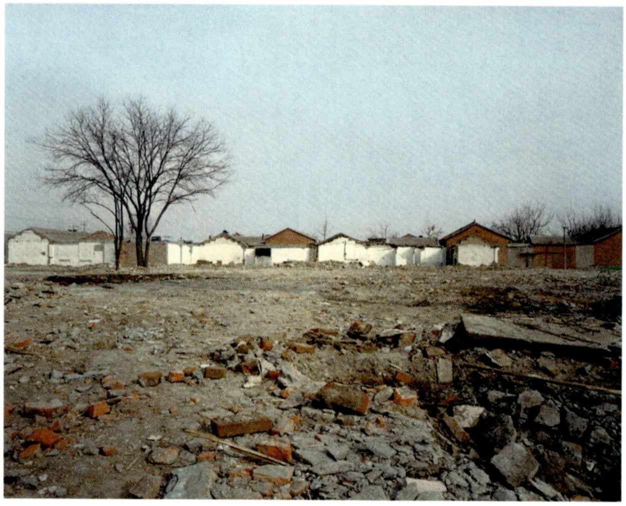
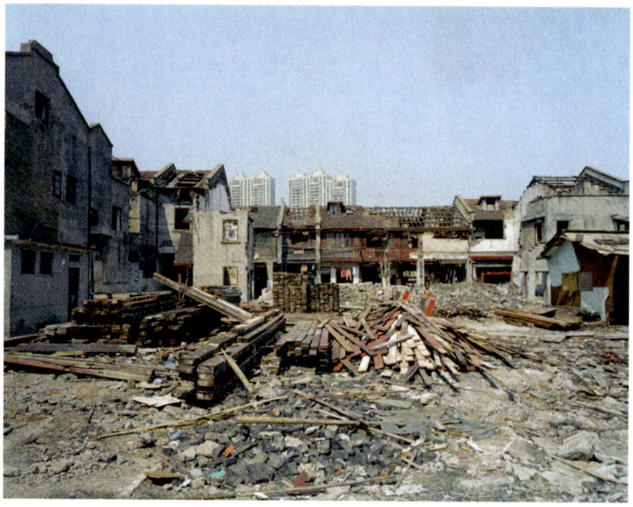

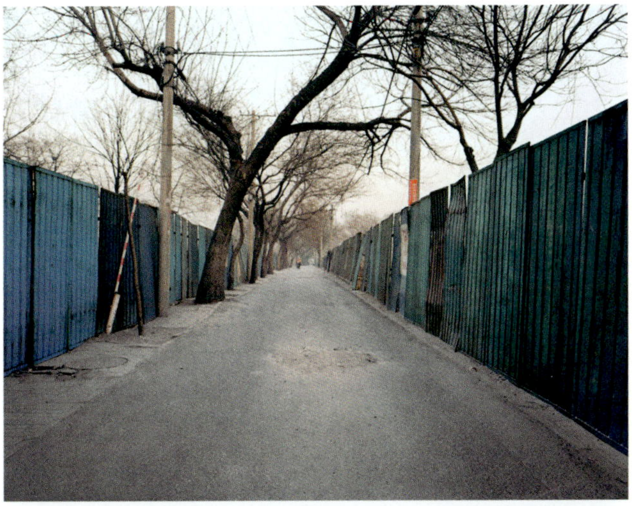

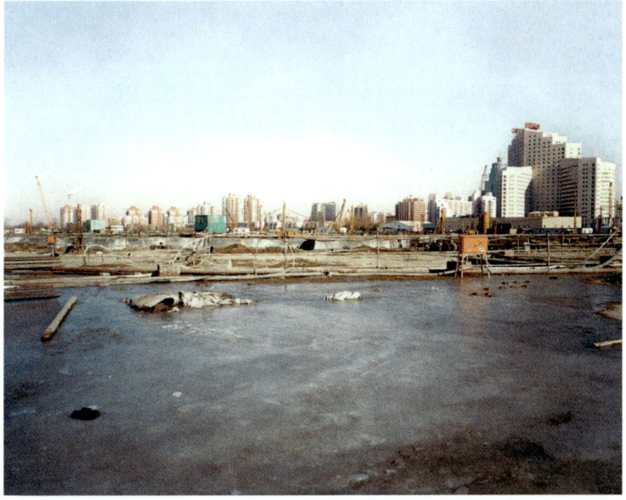

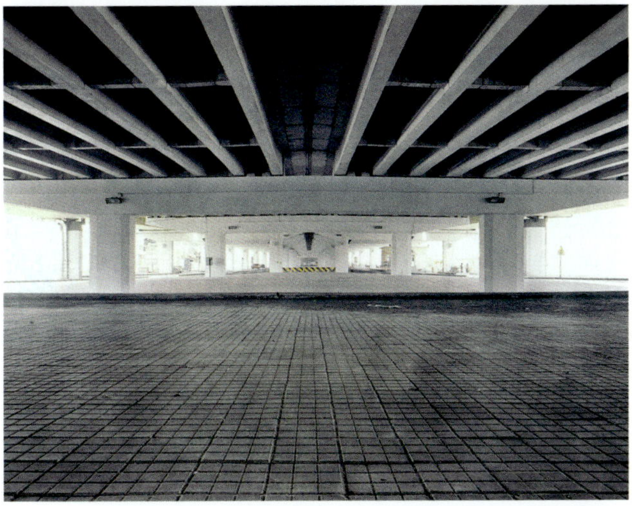

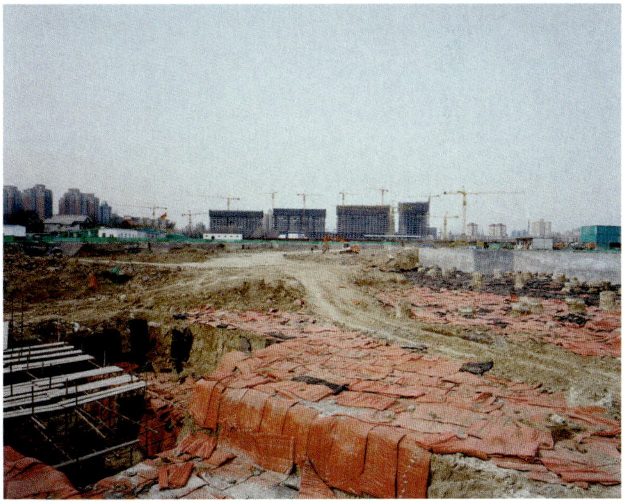

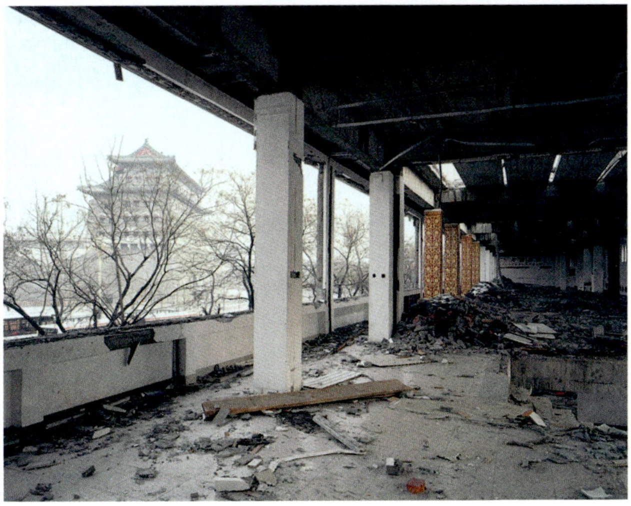

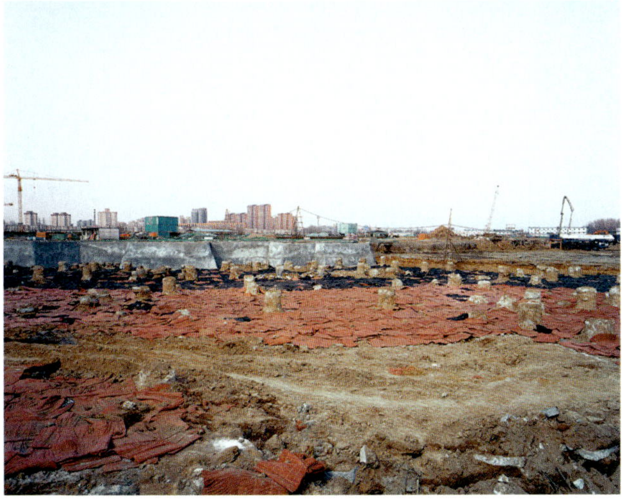

Ai Weiwei, *Provisional Landscapes*, 2002–08, series of chromogenic prints, 97 × 122 cm each

unforgettably in the series of photographs *Provisional Landscapes* (2002–08). Professionally organised archaeological digs and multiple chance discoveries resulted in the unearthing of a massive amount of material, some of it of major significance but inevitably much of low quality. In the markets of the major cities and in areas like Hollywood Road in Hong Kong, newly excavated objects of all kinds spilled out onto the pavement, still encrusted with earth. The steady accumulation of knowledge that Ai acquired through handling countless works, comparing them for quality and talking to experienced dealers who had acquired their expertise in the same way provided him with a level of discernment in classical Chinese art unusual among contemporary artists of his generation, especially one who was gaining his reputation through the publication of three books, *Black Cover Book* (1994), *White Cover Book* (1995) and *Grey Cover Book* (1997),[5] that provided up-to-date information on international developments in the visual and performing arts unavailable elsewhere in China.

The parallel development of his understanding of issues germane to the development of contemporary art in China and his growing passion for Chinese classical art may be interpreted as a natural development of the decision he made in New York to stop painting in favour of using readymade materials. In New York he used materials that were readily available – cheap manufactured objects for the most part. In China he recognised that his interest in the material culture of classical China, still in its fledgling state, could be developed into a modus operandi with enormous potential, and

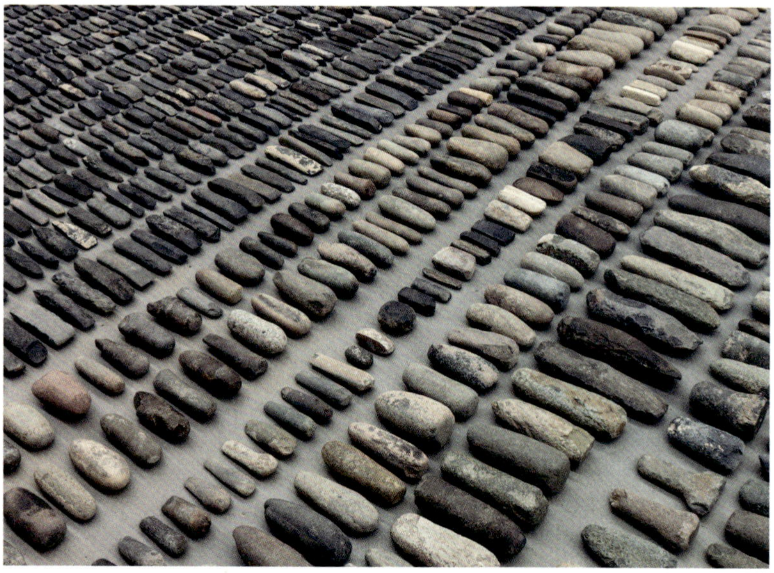

Ai Weiwei, *Still Life*, 1993–2000, installation of 3,600 stone tools dating from the Stone Age to the Shang dynasty (10,000–1100 BC)

that the material was widely available in antiques markets and in warehouses housing architectural elements from demolished buildings all over China.

Ai's interest in Chinese antiquities was not just academic. He was beginning to make small purchases for himself – stone sculpture at the beginning when nobody was interested, jades, Neolithic material and furniture – a passion that soon became an obsession. Between 1993 and 2000, for example, he acquired 3,600 Neolithic tools that he catalogued and assembled into his first major installation, *Still Life*. This led inevitably to a consideration of more practical and theoretical matters, namely questions pertaining to the issues of forgery and copying particularly as they applied to Chinese art, not because he was collecting for collecting's sake – although there was an element of that – but because he was simultaneously contemplating ways in which he might use such materials in his own art. Some years later when he was discussing the *Circle of Animals / Zodiac Heads* (2010), he remarked that 'My work is always dealing with real or fake, authenticity, what the value is, and how the value is related to current political and social understandings and misunderstandings. I think there's a strong humorous aspect there.'[6]

REAL OR FAKE

For Ai Weiwei the word 'fake' is as much part of his public persona as the gesture of giving the middle finger has been since 1995–96 when he first began using it in photographs taken in Hong Kong, Washington, DC and on Tiananmen Square. In 2003 he started his architectural office FAKE Design in the Caochangdi district of Beijing, in the studio-house he had designed for himself in 1999. It was a counter-intuitive choice of name since his unadorned, minimal structures were as pure as could be, while it was the countless apartment buildings and mansions going up all over China bedecked with mismatched classical details and fancy names that were the real fake design. The fact that the Chinese pronunciation of 'fake' sounds like the English word 'fuck' was also a strong part of its appeal, and this was soon to appear in numerous guises: in a photograph taken on Tiananmen Square in 2000 in which the letters 'FUCK' are sunburned onto his chest,[7] in neon and metal installed outside the wall of his studio, and in oil on canvas in 2004. As has happened in previous epochs in the long history of China when the production of fakes kept pace with the demands of a growing market, the period when Ai was beginning to collect and to produce works that frequently utilised his purchases coincided with a golden age in this symbiotic relationship. More than at any previous time in Chinese history,

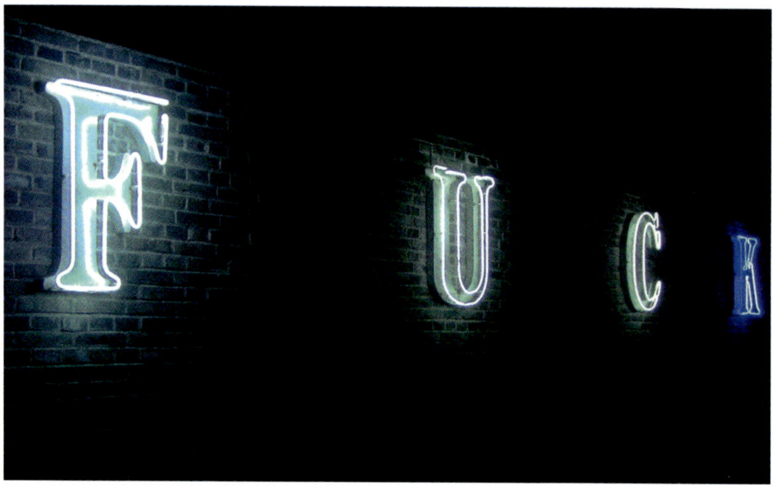

Ai Weiwei, *FUCK*, 2000, Neon installation

perhaps, the period in which Ai began using antique materials in his work was characterised by the simultaneous occurrence of a vast increase in the amount of archaeological material available and a rapidly expanding art market that resulted in unprecedented distortions of value.

Some recent exhibitions and publications clarify some of the issues that so intrigue Ai and that he has explored in a multitude of different ways.[8] In the section on 'Faking in the East' in the comprehensive exhibition *Fake? The Art of Deception* at the British Museum in 1990 it was pointed out that there was a commercial market for calligraphy in China from at least the fifth century CE and that Chinese bronzes began to be studied, exchanged and forged by the eleventh century. As the definition of what was collectible widened, so did the art market, particularly in the late Ming period of the sixteenth and seventeenth centuries and in late Imperial and Republican China, where the scale of art forgery was 'massive'.[9] However, in any discussion of the role of copying and forgery in China in comparison with attitudes in the West, there must be a major caveat as the concept of copying has a long and respectable history in China, particularly in painting, where it is normal practice for an aspiring painter to copy the works of ancient masters in order to fully understand them and ultimately subtly transform them into personal statements. As is to be expected, different practices and expectations prevail in ceramics[10] and sculpture, both of which are of enormous importance to Ai in his artistic practice.

Ai gained first-hand knowledge of the manufacture of porcelain through his friendship with Liu Weiwei, owner of the kiln in Jingdezhen where subsequently he was to do a great deal of work, making frequent visits there from the mid-1990s onwards.

A centre of pottery production for over 1,700 years and later for the production of porcelain for the Imperial court, Jingdezhen had fallen on hard times after the creation of the People's Republic of China (PRC) in 1949, all but two of its state-run factories having been shut down. Soon revived with an infusion of capital from Taiwan and Hong Kong, it began producing porcelain on an industrial scale, as well as remarkably high-quality fakes that infested the market. The British Museum exhibition already referred to displayed a Ming dynasty bowl and a copy side by side and commented that the 'modern copies are easily identified, not only from their slightly inferior painting but above all from their very thick and clumsy potting'.[11] That is no longer the case. Scholars have commented that even with all the latest scientific methods of analysis at their disposal and months of deliberations, modern copies are frequently of such high quality that it can be next to impossible to distinguish them from originals.[12]

Unlike the traditional collecting categories already mentioned, sculpture in stone had never been a focus of collectors in China. Valued more for its iconography than its aesthetic qualities, it had frequently been subject to vandalism over many centuries, and often existed in fragmentary form, generally without provenance. That being said, Chinese sculpture became a subject of intense interest to international scholars in the early years of the twentieth century, but even then it appears probable that imitations were produced as soon as new material was unearthed. In the exhibition *Chinese Buddhist Sculpture in a New Light* at the Freer Gallery of Art in Washington, DC in 2002, one of the works examined in depth was a red sandstone stela, dated by inscription to 521 CE of the Northern Wei dynasty (386–534 CE). The author noted that 'In the early part of the twentieth century, dealers in the Xi'an area sold both Chinese antiquities and modern works made to look like ancient sculpture. This means that examples of genuine Northern Wei sculpture were available to guide modern fabrications. In such a situation, the best-made works of modern sculpture cannot easily be differentiated from those that are genuinely old. It is now widely believed that many works of Chinese sculpture sold by Yamanaka and Company [a pioneering international dealer in Asian art], from whom the Freer purchased its stela, were modern fabrications.'[13]

More recently, a major hoard of Buddhist sculpture dating from 527–577 CE was discovered in Qingzhou, Shandong province. As in the early years of the twentieth century, this led to a proliferation of contemporary copies that soon infiltrated the market, a major difference being that buyers were now as likely to be Chinese as foreigners, a revival of Buddhism and contemporary decorating trends leading to a re-evaluation by newly affluent collectors in China.[14]

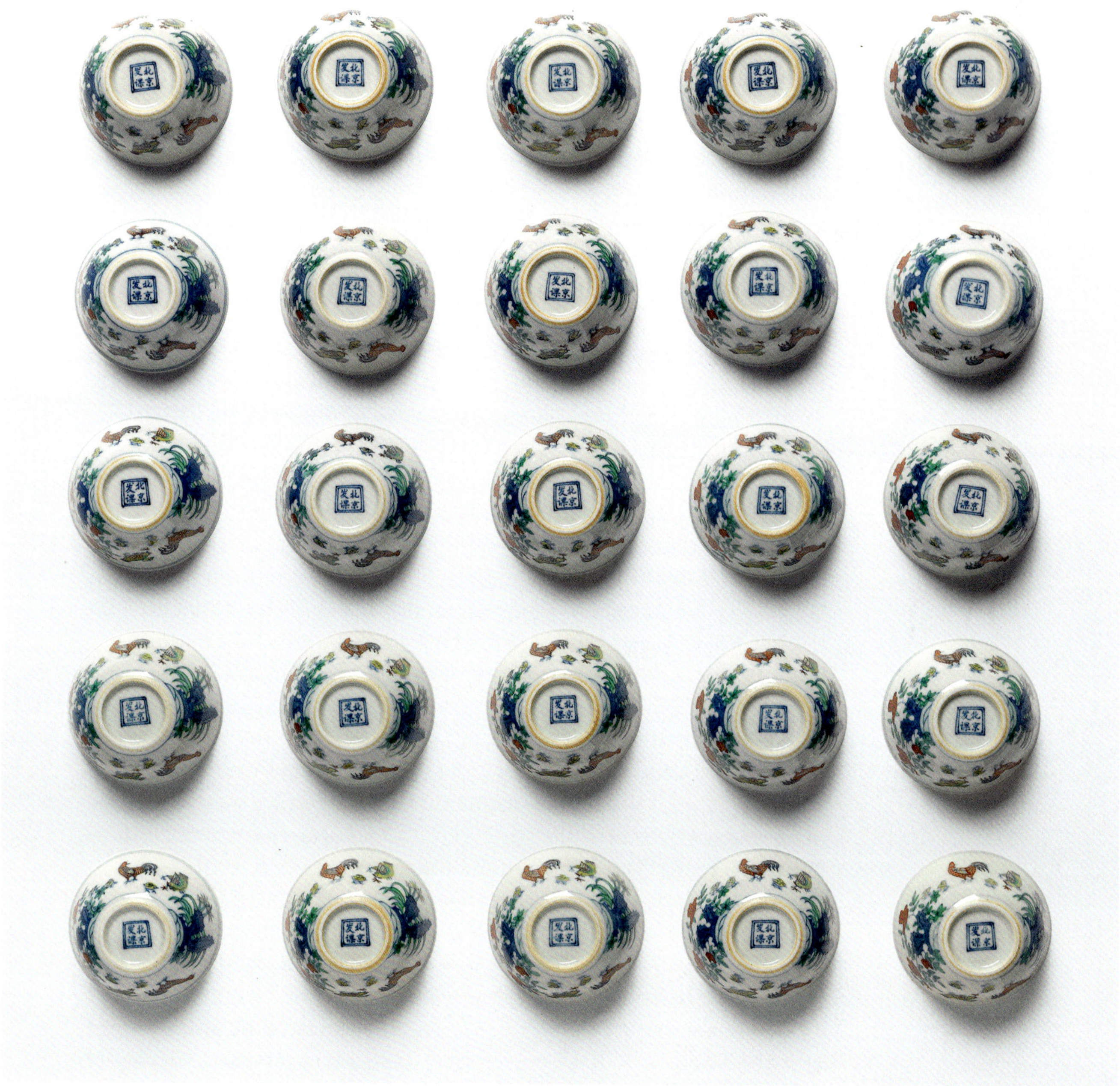

Ai Weiwei, *Chicken Cup*, 2015, installation of 25 porcelain reproductions of a Chenghua period (1464–87) 'chicken cup', marked 'Beijing Fake' on bottom

On the subject of value, Ai Weiwei once wrote that ‘Like walking at the seaside, if you see a pretty shell you might collect one or two, or you’ll pick up a few interesting stones. A chair that has been passed down over hundreds of years will similarly arouse your curiosity. You can observe the chair and imagine the postures of previous generations, but I wouldn’t advocate it or flaunt it for this reason. I don’t believe that aside from being able to satisfy my curiosity, such a chair has any genuine value. In most circumstances there is no one influencing me. I have many books and a decent understanding of ancient Chinese vessels, no matter if they are wooden, bronze, or jade. But most of my efforts go into forgetting these things, avoiding taking the same path, or saying what has already been said, and attempting to contribute a new way of looking at the situation in everything I do.’[15] He later stated: ‘You have to find an old photo, or an old piece of jade, or an old piece of a root. From the root you can imagine what the tree was like.’[16]

Needless to say, Ai Weiwei’s attitude was not the prevailing one during the time when the market for classical Chinese art was growing exponentially worldwide. The model provided by the international auction houses was adopted by Chinese start-ups, which rapidly gained ground, although a lack of expertise and regulation at the beginning resulted in some unsettling irregularities that severely skewed the market. Instead of being a field in which scholarly appreciation dominated as in the past, it became a field of rampant speculation. The market was flooded by forgeries, and many of the record prices that were achieved at auction, such as $64.5 million paid for an ink painting by Qi Baishi at China Guardian, Beijing in May 2011, did not survive scrutiny, as two years after the auction the buyer had not paid.[17]

Paralleling this phenomenon was a museum building drive, with periodic announcements of completed projects. With officials obliged to fill up newly created public buildings, acquisitions were often made in a hurry. According to official statistics, between 2016 and 2020 a museum opened every two days in China, and at least three were closed down as most of the works on display were forgeries.[18]

On 8 March 2014, a Chenghua period (1464–87) ‘chicken cup’ sold for HK$281.24 million (US$36.05 million) to a collector who was photographed sipping tea from it after the auction, a gesture that some commentators regarded as not in the best of taste. Although it is generally thought that no more than 12 such original cups have survived, many more soon entered the market ‘with varying degrees of verisimilitude’, as Stacey Pierson remarked dryly.[19]

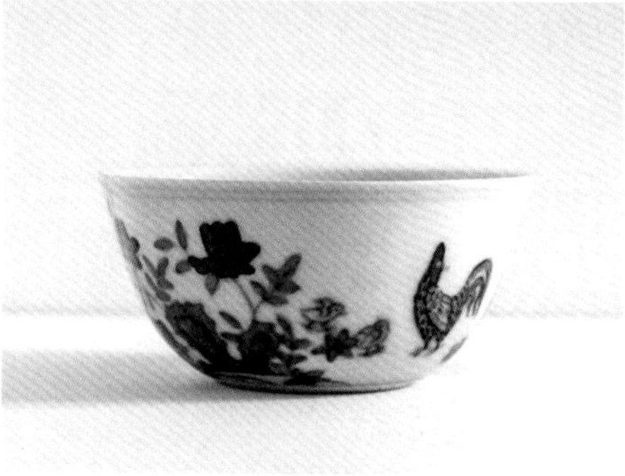

Ai Weiwei, *Chicken Cup*, 2015, one of 25 porcelain reproductions of a Chenghua period (1464–87) 'chicken cup', marked 'Beijing Fake' on bottom

In 2015 Ai responded to this transaction with characteristic aplomb, presenting a group of 25 exact replicas upside down in a vitrine, each one marked 'Beijing Fake' on the bottom, showing that the technique for making them was still going strong.

Very often the record prices achieved at auction for Chinese works of art during this period had nothing to do with aesthetic or historical value. Flaunting of newly acquired wealth and the urge to be seen repatriating part of the national patrimony from overseas auctions were perhaps more significant. In a discussion of the frenzy that erupted every time one of the 12 bronze heads from the zodiac fountain in the Yuanming Yuan appeared at auction, Ai commented that 'they're not worth that much, and they're not Chinese and they're not national treasures. So all this talk of national treasures being looted by Westerners, and now buying it back – it's political hype ... They're just like a toilet seat or anything else.'[20]

DROPPING, APPROPRIATING, ACCUMULATING, REPLICATING

Originally used by Ai Weiwei in a recent interview, the notion of 'the liberty of doubt', the freedom to question, is taken for granted in Cambridge but not everywhere in the world, as he knows only too well.[21] He has himself experienced the penalties for questioning orthodoxy in a totalitarian society, beginning with the years between 1958 and 1976 mostly spent in harsh circumstances in Xinjiang, where his father had been exiled. An outsider in his New York years, Ai suppressed any explicit statements of discontent, but the radical nature of his political and ethical position could be read into the relatively small number of works produced in his first decade back in Beijing. After 2000, his range of activities expanded to include video and architecture, culminating in his collaboration with Herzog & de Meuron on the design of the National Stadium for the Beijing Summer Olympic Games in 2008.

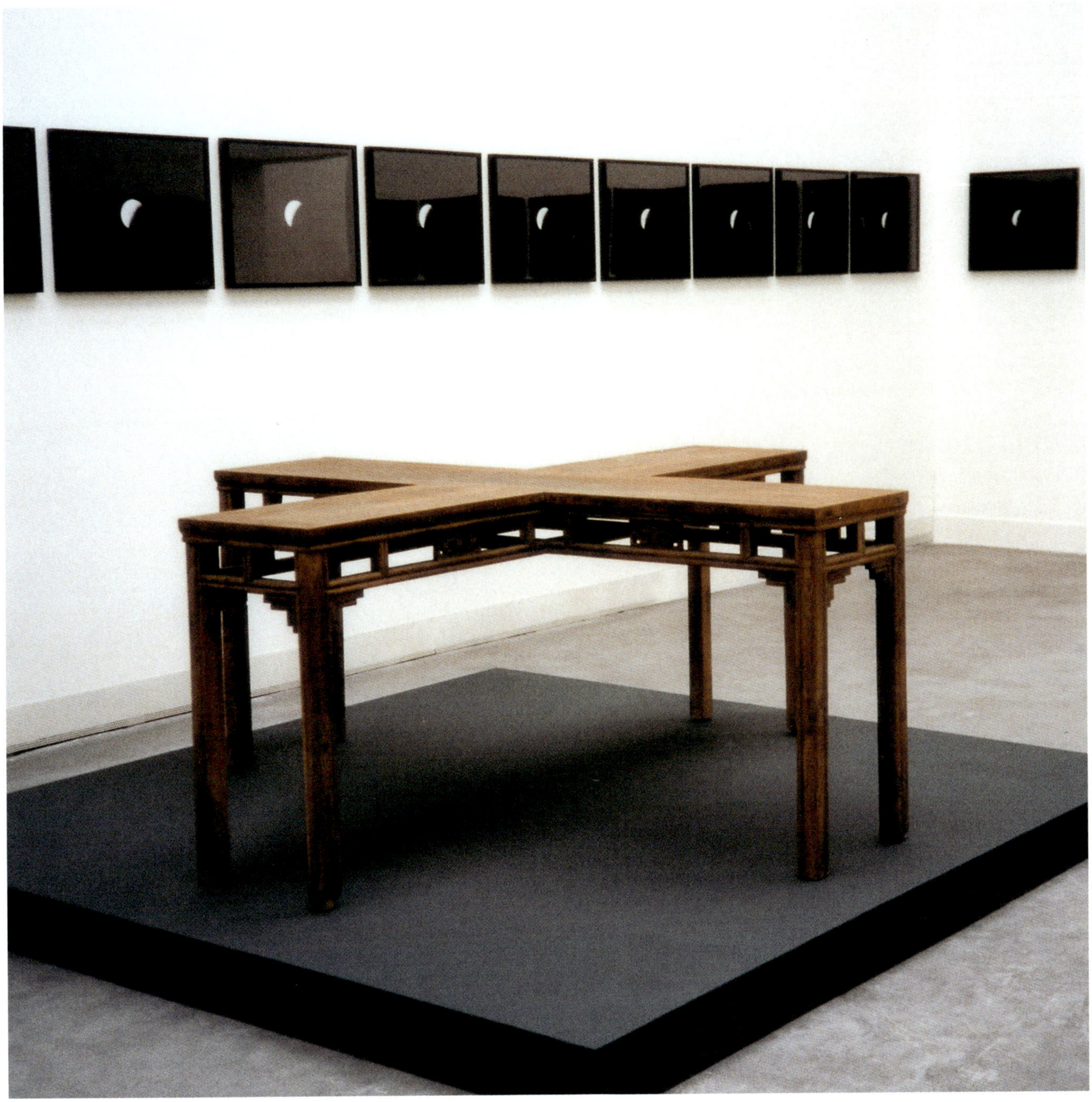

Ai Weiwei, *Crossed Tables*, 1998, Qing dynasty tables, 86 × 113.5 × 206 cm

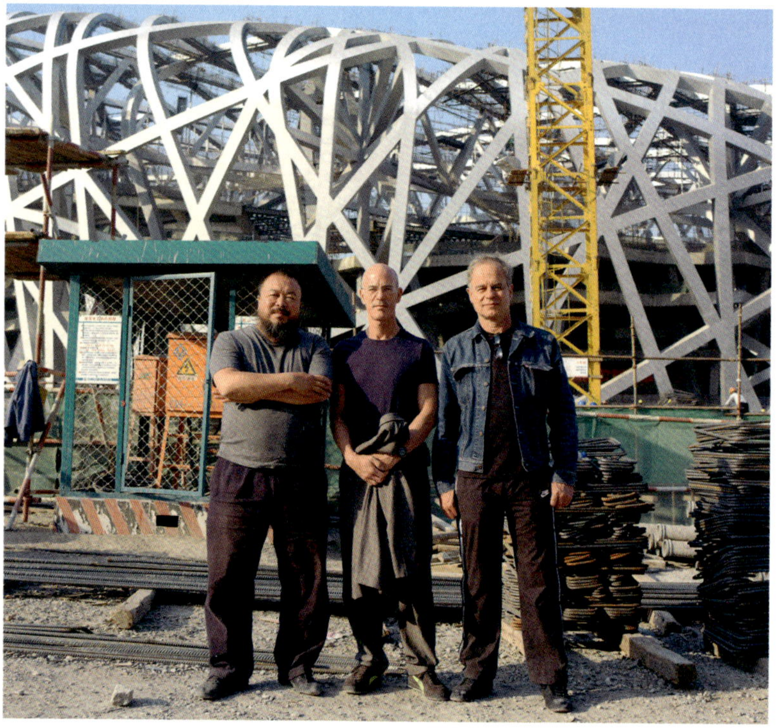

Ai Weiwei with Jacques Herzog and Pierre de Meuron, National Stadium (Bird's Nest) for the 2008 Summer Olympic Games in Beijing, 2005–08

The increasingly exasperated comments on Ai's blog on the chauvinism of the Olympic celebrations and the government ineptitude and prevarication in the handling of the Sichuan earthquake on 12 May 2008 led to an inevitable showdown. His blog was closed down and on 3 April 2011 he was arrested, spending the next 81 days in secret detention. Unable to travel for the next four years, he used the time to plan an unrivalled series of international exhibitions – not in China, of course – as a way of showing the authorities that he was a free man in spite of everything. Much of his work since 2015, when he moved to Berlin, is centred on the worldwide refugee crisis, censorship and associated social problems, as can be seen from the selection of works in porcelain, jade, marble and wood in the smaller gallery at Kettle's Yard.

As is always the case, the installation at Kettle's Yard has been meticulously prepared by Ai and his studio in order to make sure that although many of the works have been previously exhibited elsewhere, they speak to each other as if for the first time and relate to the given space. Ai places the Chinese sculptures he purchased at auction in elegant display cases that he designed and uses for his own works – that is to say, he accords them all equal importance, even though in some cases there are doubts about authenticity. Innocent until proven guilty, he seems to be saying.

Beginning with *Still Life* and *Whitewash* (both 1993–2000) and continuing with such works as *Feet* (2003), *White Stone Axes* (2006) and *Spouts* (2015), he has previously exhibited groups of ancient objects and fragments under his own name. While of little value in themselves in the marketplace, they attain substantial value when they become listed as works by Ai Weiwei. At Kettle's Yard he does not take that step, choosing to allow them to exist in their own right, even though their provenance and date of execution will probably never be known with absolute certainty. As antiquities 'in exile', there is perhaps an allegorical connection to the refugees whose plight has been Ai's primary focus since 2015. Ai values the antique sculptures regardless of their provenance. On the part of the viewer, unlikely to be an expert in the field, this encourages prolonged looking and speculation. The journey from Shaanxi province to the comfort of Kettle's Yard is a long and tortuous one, and the search for proper identity papers is not yet over.

The Chinese sculptures share the larger gallery with a 2015 version of *Dropping a Han Dynasty Urn* (2005), probably the first time that LEGO bricks have crossed the threshold of Kettle's Yard. Certainly one of Ai's most celebrated works,[22] this act of the artist calmly dropping a Han dynasty (202 BCE–220 CE) urn was performed in private in the the courtyard house in Beijing where he lived, and was first published in the *White Cover Book* in 1995. Although the image was already powerful, its impact was diluted by distracting irregular patches on the brick wall behind the artist and glimpses of other parts of the house, a window on the right and a sunlit courtyard

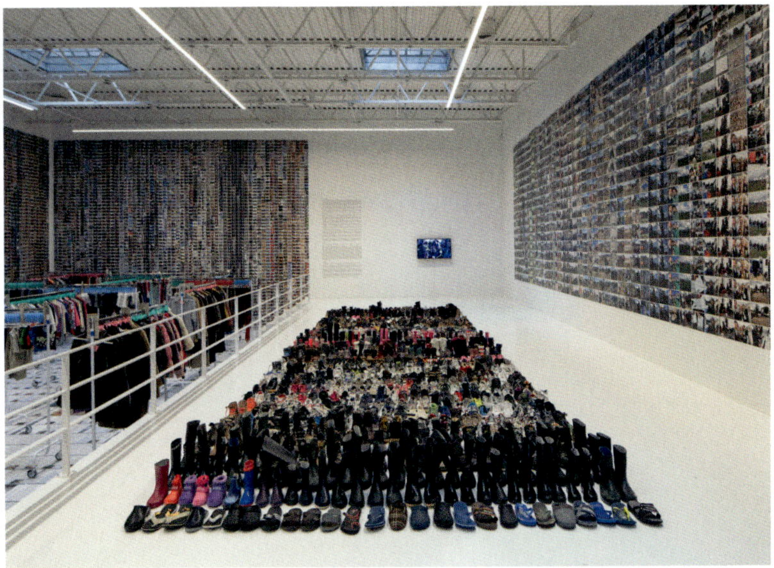

Ai Weiwei, *Laundromat*, 2016, 40 clothing racks, 2,046 clothing items, installation view, Jeffrey Deitch, New York, 2016

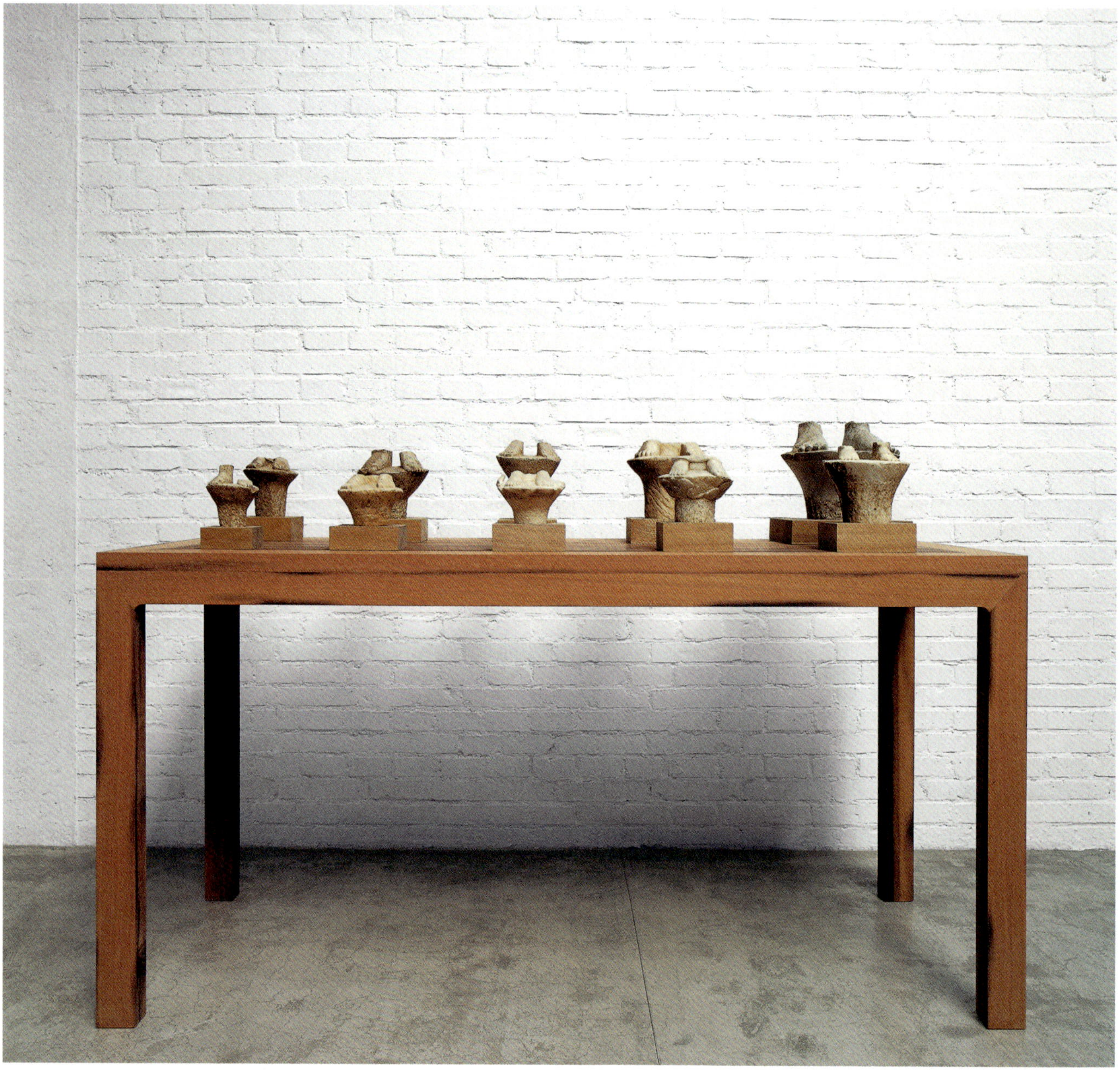

Ai Weiwei, *Feet*, fragments of stone sculpture from the Northern Qi period (550–577 CE) with individual wooden plinths and wooden table on the left. Under the title *Accidental Dropping*, it was included in the exhibition *Fuck Off* in Shanghai in 2000 that Ai curated with Feng Boyi.

Once the image had been cropped and subsequently enlarged for exhibition purposes, the deliberate nature of the act became inescapable. Although Ai has confirmed that it was indeed an ancient vessel that he dropped, doubts have been raised in some circles. It has also been suggested that the vessel was 'priceless', although in fact Han dynasty pottery was never highly valued by collectors, and at the time that Ai acquired the one he dropped they were widely available in the antiques markets for very low prices. As for his motivation, uncooperative and scornful of shibboleths as he is, he has never been a vandal, rather the opposite. He has not denied that the decision to perform this surprising act may refer to the destructive frenzy of the Cultural Revolution (1966–76), but this is one among many possible meanings. In a recent question and answer session he was asked if he still felt the same way about the destruction of cultural artefacts as he did in the 1990s, to which he replied, 'My work has a solid understanding, but at the same time, it happens intuitively. It cannot be repeated or clearly defined by the author.'[23] Ai's work always operates on multiple levels, the personal, the aesthetic and the political. Perhaps being deliberately provocative, he has recently referred to this iconic work as 'a capricious, inane act' in which he introduced his brother Ai Dan to the 'continuous capture function of one of my cameras' as he let the earthenware urn fall from his hands.[24] The viewer is offered multiple choices!

With a deep respect for the achievements of Chinese artists and craftspeople of the past, and mindful of the survival of many of their skills in spite of the political turbulence of the last century, Ai has created a considerable body of work that explores this complex territory. If the urn-dropping performance might be seen as a declaration of independence or a clearing of the air, the *Vault-of-Heaven Vase* (1997) demonstrated that in collaboration with a skilled craftsperson, a late twentieth-century artist could create a vase that is virtually indistinguishable from its ancestor. Comparable vases were being sold at auction for record prices at the time. Twenty years later, this unmatched collaboration resulted in another emanation from the past, the *Dragon Vase* (2017). Just the year before, a blue-and-white dragon jar of the Ming dynasty (1368–1644) had sold for HK$158 million at Christie's in Hong Kong, having been used as an umbrella stand by its former owner, an unintended parallel of Marcel Duchamp's idea for a 'reverse readymade', 'to take a Rembrandt and use it like an ironing board'. An anomaly visible only to those knowledgeable in Chinese history is the addition of a sixth claw to the dragon, one more than the number allowed to the

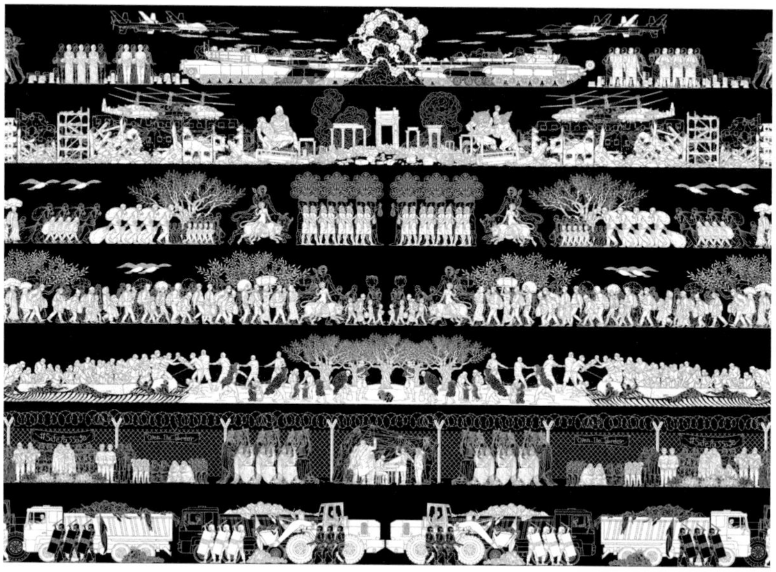

Ai Weiwei, *Odyssey*, 2016, wallpaper print

emperor. In China in the twenty-first century it is not the number of claws that leads to severe punishment but incorrect political thoughts, 'picking quarrels and making trouble'.[25]

Another approach can be seen in *Han Dynasty Urn with Coca-Cola Logo*, a 2014 version of a work dating from 1994, exhibited next to a Chinese painted Han dynasty 'cocoon' vase. Painted in flowering cursive script on an authentic but by no means rare Han dynasty vase, the Coca-Cola logo declares its intent without concealing what lies underneath, as is the case in the series of painted vases not represented in this exhibition. While appreciating their cultural value, for Ai they are just 'ready-mades'.[26]

Although the emphasis in the exhibition *The Liberty of Doubt* is on Ai's ongoing investigation of questions of authenticity and value in the field of Chinese antiquities and cultural heritage, it is clear that this does not exist separately from his works dealing with current political and social issues. Rather, it is the same inquiring mindset that characterises both, rejecting received ideas regarding the valuation and categorisation of antiquities in the former and unthinking acceptance of political dogmas and tolerance of injustice in the latter. The refined medium of porcelain, valued for centuries for both its decorative and utilitarian qualities, has been transformed into a vehicle for expressing powerful political messages. *Brain Inflation* (2012) is a porcelain plate showing the brain scan image belonging to Ai, who had been beaten up by the police in Chengdu when he went to testify on behalf of Tan Zuoren, an activist who was seeking information on the collapse of numerous school buildings after the Sichuan earthquake in 2008. Seen from a distance, the set of six *Blue-and-White Porcelain Plates* (2017) has the decorative splendour of the finest porcelain produced in Jingdezhen for the Imperial court, but close inspection reveals tragic imagery of scenes of war and ruins, crossing oceans and refugee camps mingled with comparable scenes from the ancient world.

The Chair for Non-attendance (2013) and the threatening *Surveillance Camera with Plinth* (2014) overlook an early twentieth-century display case, its traditional proportions contrasting with Ai's elegantly austere vitrines. As is often the case in Ai's work, the smaller works in porcelain, marble and jade refer to events in his personal history that reflect broader socio-political conditions. Endowed with a multitude of positive qualities and values in Chinese culture, jade is co-opted to form *Handcuffs* (2011), made shortly after his release from his 81-day confinement in an unknown location in 2011. It is also used to endow a sex toy and a set of cosmetic bottles, purchased on his behalf in New York while Ai was forbidden to leave China, with an unexpected aura of cultural gravitas. Highest-quality marble is used to transform a roll of toilet paper into a sleek modernist sculpture commemorating the moment at the beginning of the Covid-19 pandemic when this indispensable hygienic material began disappearing from supermarket shelves. Helmets entered Ai's world of forms in the aftermath of the Sichuan earthquake, and photographs show him wearing one standing in the ruins of his Shanghai studio after it had been demolished by the local authorities in 2011.

Ai Weiwei's unorthodox exhibition provides valuable insights into the complexity of his thinking and artistic practice. Rather than choosing a more familiar approach, he has chosen to raise a multitude of questions by exhibiting alongside his own works a group of 14 fragmentary Chinese sculptures that in normal circumstances would not be under such intense scrutiny as they are now. Their moment in the sun may not result in lasting readmittance to the world of the fully authenticated and accepted, but nonetheless they have served a valuable function. The exhibition does not offer easy satisfactions, posing instead questions in the public sphere that Ai Weiwei is always asking himself, not only about authenticity and how it might be defined in different cultures, and about value and how it is determined by extraneous social and economic trends, but about how to engage in a responsible manner with a world that seems to be hurtling out of control. Practising 'the liberty of doubt' is a good first step.

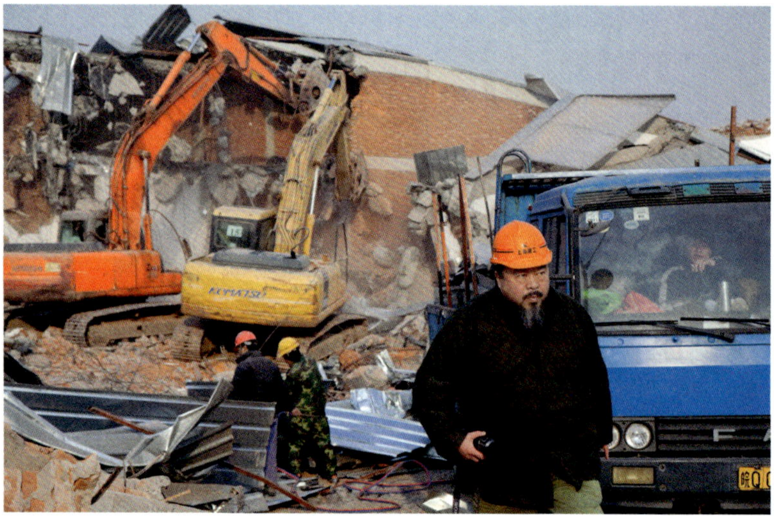

Ai Weiwei during the demolition of his Shanghai studio, 2011

1 Undated manuscript, Kettle's Yard archive, Cambridge.

2 Ronald Reagan, 'Farewell Address to the Nation', 11 January 1989.

3 *The Shock of the New* by Robert Hughes, BBC series, 1980.

4 Ai Weiwei, John Tancock and Stephanie H. Tung, *Ai Weiwei: Beijing Photographs 1993–2003*, MIT Press, Cambridge MA, 2018, pp.68, 70, 73.

5 Ai Weiwei, *Black Cover Book* (1994), *White Cover Book* (1995) and *Grey Cover Book* (1997), artist's books published by Tai Tei Publishing Company Limited, Hong Kong.

6 Susan Delson (ed), *Circle of Animals*, Prestel, Munich and London, 2011, p.59.

7 Ai, Tancock and Tung, *op. cit.*, p.235.

8 *Authentic: Truth and Perception in Chinese Art*, Philadelphia Museum of Art, on display until 3 July 2022.

9 Mark Jones (ed), *Fake? The Art of Deception*, exhibition catalogue, British Museum, London, 1990, pp.99–100. 'The acts of falsifying, replicating and altering artefacts in China are intimately connected with the growth of what has been called a "rare art tradition". This has taken the form of the gradual expansion of the commodity market, in which different groups of artefacts come to be privileged as "art", acquiring significance as concentrated cultural and economic capital. First to achieve this was calligraphy, for which there was a commercial market from at least the fifth century AD … The archaic vessels of the Chinese Bronze Age, although accumulated as numinous treasures under the early empire, did not fully achieve the status of "collectables" until the eleventh century, when they too began to be studied, exchanged as commodities and forged. But it was the sixteenth and early seventeenth centuries, in the highly commercial world of the late Ming, which saw the widest expansion in the activities of the Chinese collector, and with it an upsurge in the manufacture of fraudulent antiquities and works of art to feed a market larger than could be satisfied by the limited supply of genuine items.'

10 Stacey Pierson, 'True or False? Defining the Fake in Chinese Porcelain', *Les Cahiers de Framespa*, no.31, 2019, https://doi.org/10.4000/framespa.6168. 'One of the challenges of investigating faking as a concept and practice in Chinese ceramics is the fluid nature of the word "fake" in Chinese language and English.' The philosopher Byung-Chul Han notes that 'the Chinese have two different concepts of a copy. *Fangzhipin* are imitations where the difference from the original is obvious. These are small models or copies that can be purchased in a museum shop, for example. The second concept for a copy is *fuzhipin*. They are exact reproductions of the original which, for the Chinese, are of equal value to the original … The discrepancy with regard to the understanding of what a copy is has often led to misunderstandings and arguments between China and Western museums. The Chinese often send copies abroad instead of originals, in the firm belief that they are not essentially different

from the originals. The rejection that then comes from the Western museums is perceived by the Chinese as an insult.' Byung-Chul Han, *Shanzhai: Deconstruction in Chinese*, MIT Press, Cambridge MA, 2017, pp.60–61.

11 Jones (ed), *op. cit.*, p.38, no.13.

12 Conversation with Dr Alfreda Murck, curator at the Metropolitan Museum of Art, New York, 1978–91, currently associated with the Department of Art History and Archaeology, Columbia University, New York.

13 Stanley K. Abe, *A Freer Stela Reconsidered*, Freer Gallery of Art and Arthur M. Sackler Gallery Occasional Papers, Smithsonian Institution, Washington, DC, 2003, vol.3, pp.37–38, published on the occasion of the special exhibition *Chinese Buddhist Sculpture in a New Light*, 14 April – 4 May 2003.

14 Conversation with Jin Xu, Assistant Professor of Art at Vassar College, Poughkeepsie, New York.

15 Ai Weiwei, *So Sorry*, exhibition catalogue, Haus der Kunst, Munich, 2009, p.20.

16 Ai Weiwei, *Raiz*, exhibition catalogue, Oca, Parque Ibirapuera, São Paulo, 2018, p.148.

17 See David Barboza, Graham Bowley and Amanda Cox, 'A Culture of Bidding: Forging an Art Market in China', *New York Times*, 28 October 2013.

18 'Over 1,000 New Museums Open in China during Past 5 Years', https://news.cgtn.com, 26 July 2021. 'A new museum opened in China every two days on average over the past five years with the total number of museums nationwide rising from 4,692 in 2016 to 5,788 in 2020 according to official data released on Saturday.' After discoveries of fakes in their collections, Jiboazhai Museum in Hebei province closed in 2013, and Lucheng Museum in Liaoning Province in 2014. Chongqing University Art Museum closed for investigation in 2019, shortly after opening.

19 Pierson, *op. cit.*

20 Delson, *op. cit.*, p.57.

21 Interview with Ai Weiwei, Films4Transparency, 19th IACC (International Anti-Corruption Conference), online: https://vimeo.com/487592048.

22 Dario Gamboni, 'Portrait of the Artist as an Iconoclast', in *Ai Weiwei: Dropping the Urn (Ceramic Works, 5000 BCE – 2010 CE)*, ed. Gregg Moore, exhibition catalogue, Arcadia University Art Gallery, Glenside, Pennsylvania, 2010, p.86. 'The fame and the image of Ai Weiwei remain primarily associated with the iconoclastic component of his art and especially his 1995 triptych *Dropping a Han Dynasty Urn*.'

23 Tim Lewis, 'Ai Weiwei: An Artist Must Be an Activist', *The Guardian*, 22 March 2020.

24 Ai Weiwei, *1000 Years of Joys and Sorrows: A Memoir*, Crown, New York, p.199.

25 Clause from Article 293 of the 1997 revision of the People's Republic of China's penal code, maximum sentence five years, often used against human rights activists.

26 Edward Spencer-Churchill, Julian Schnabel, Emma Crichton-Miller *et al.*, *Ai Weiwei at Blenheim Palace*, exhibition catalogue, Blenheim Palace, Woodstock, Oxfordshire, 2015, p.68.

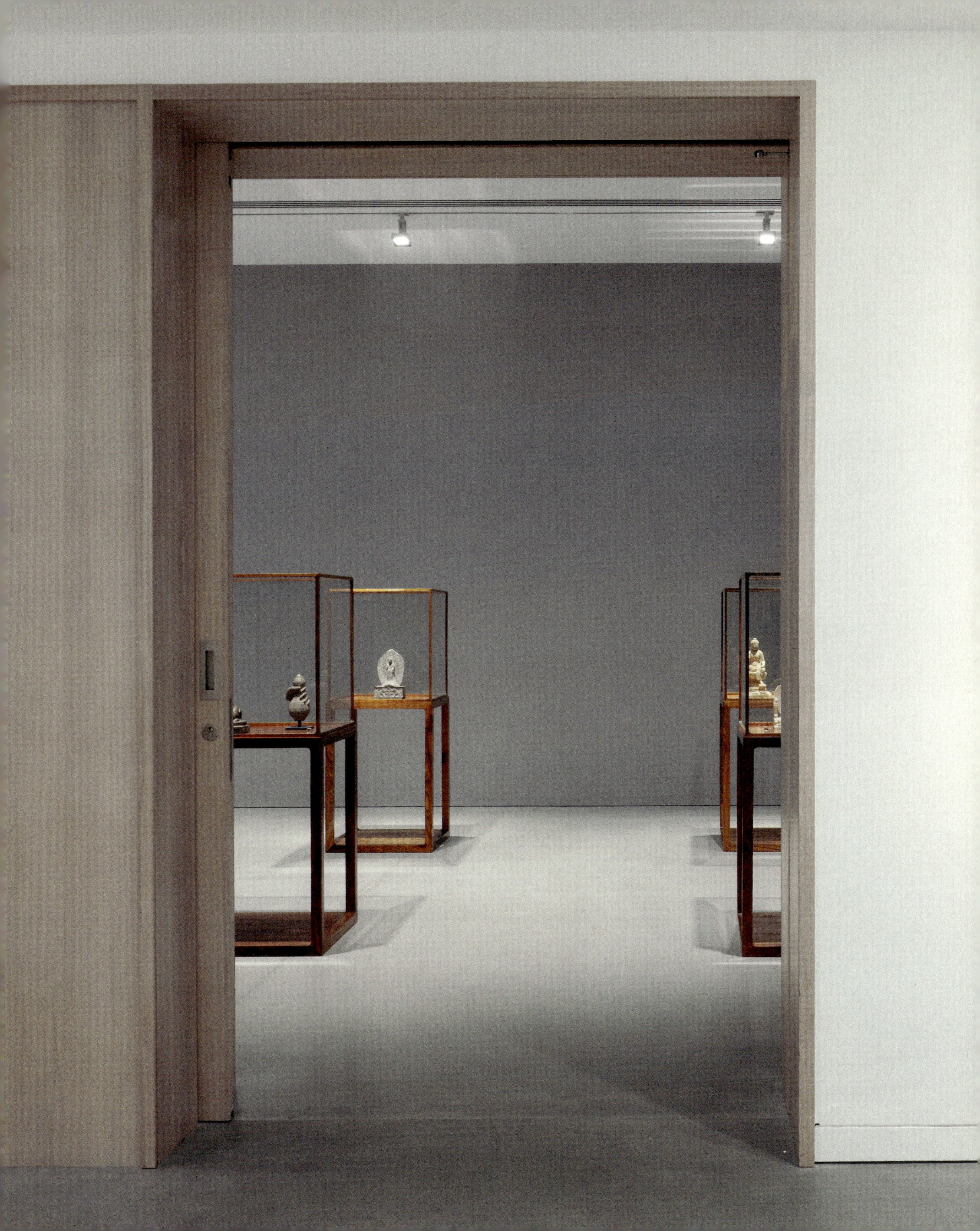

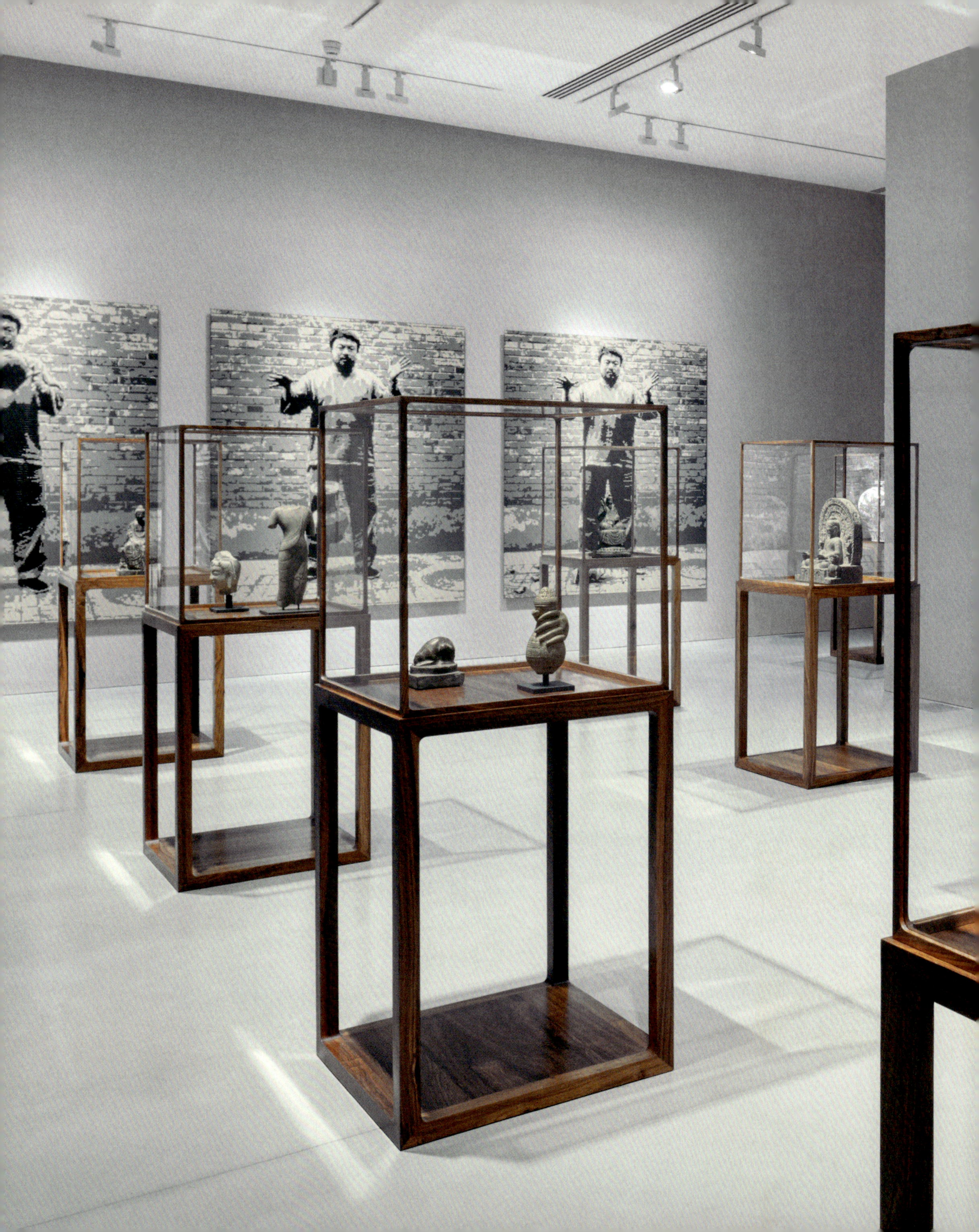

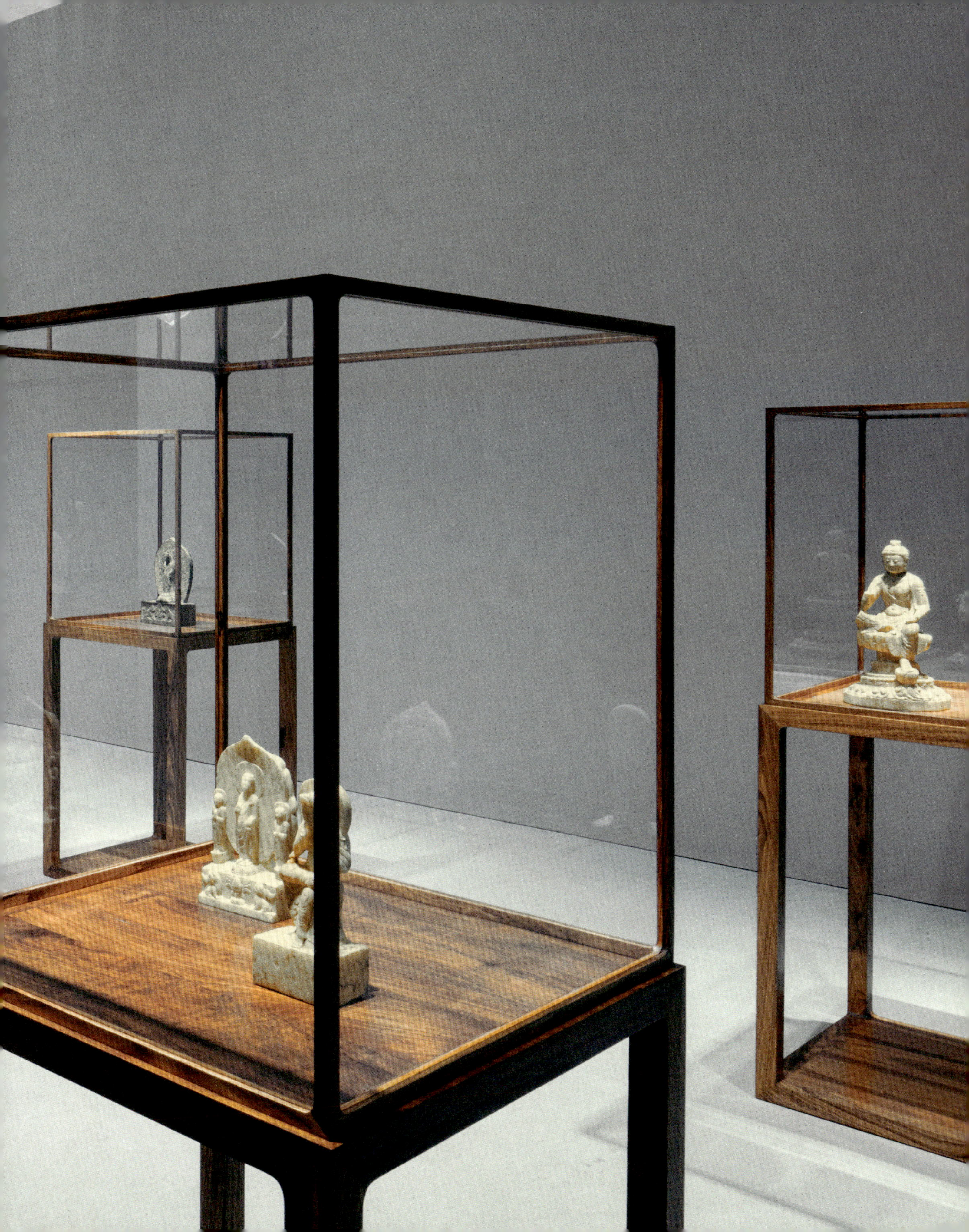

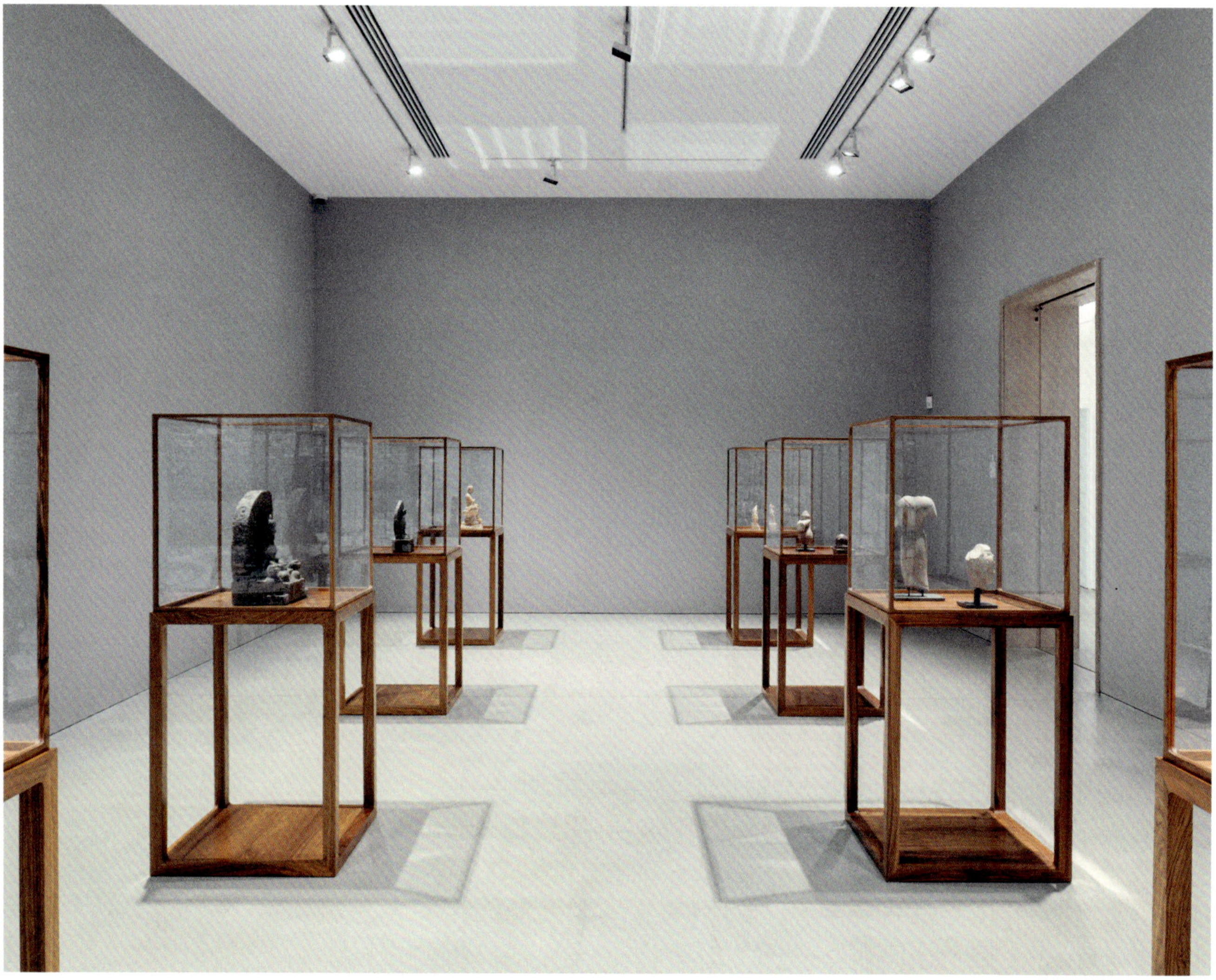

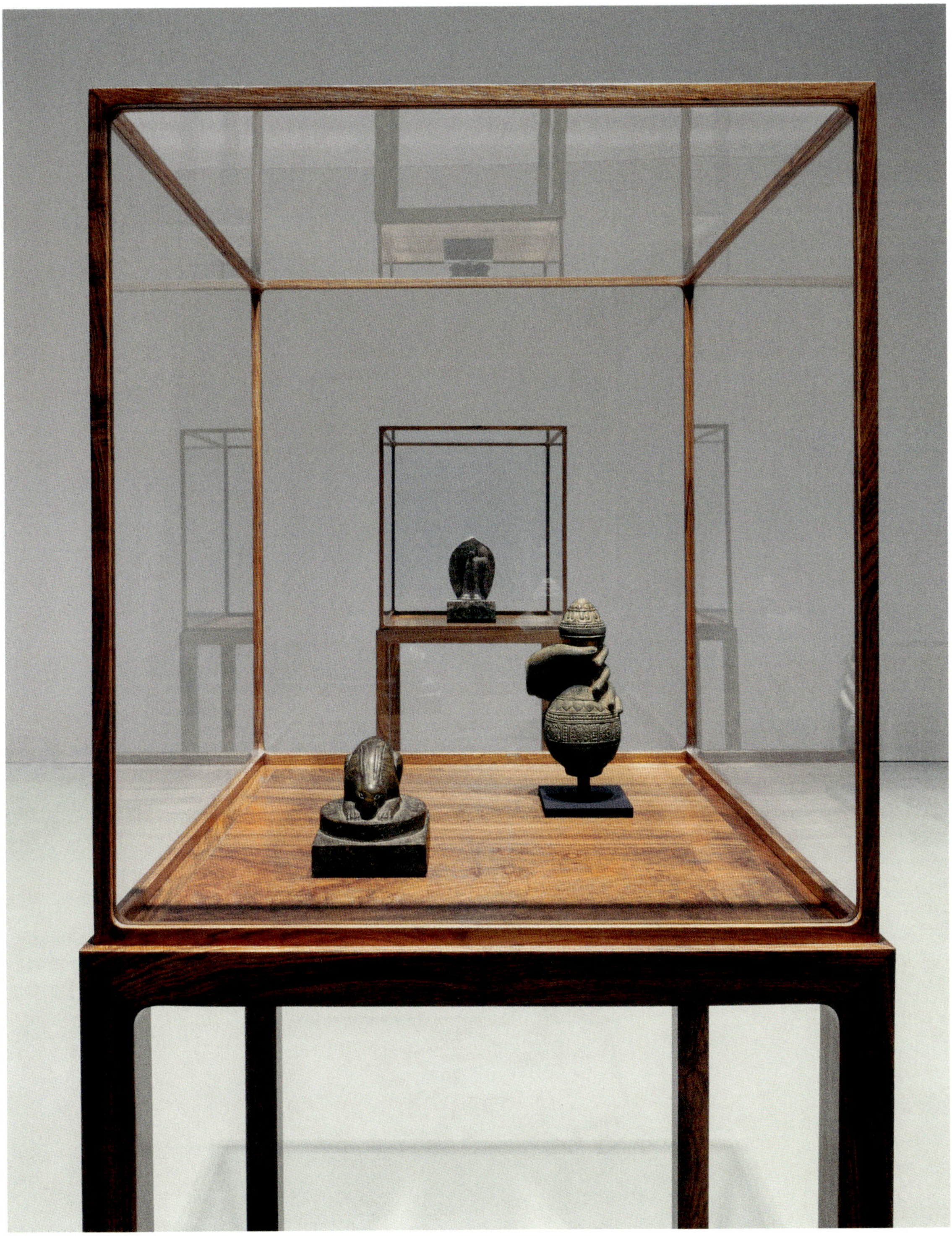

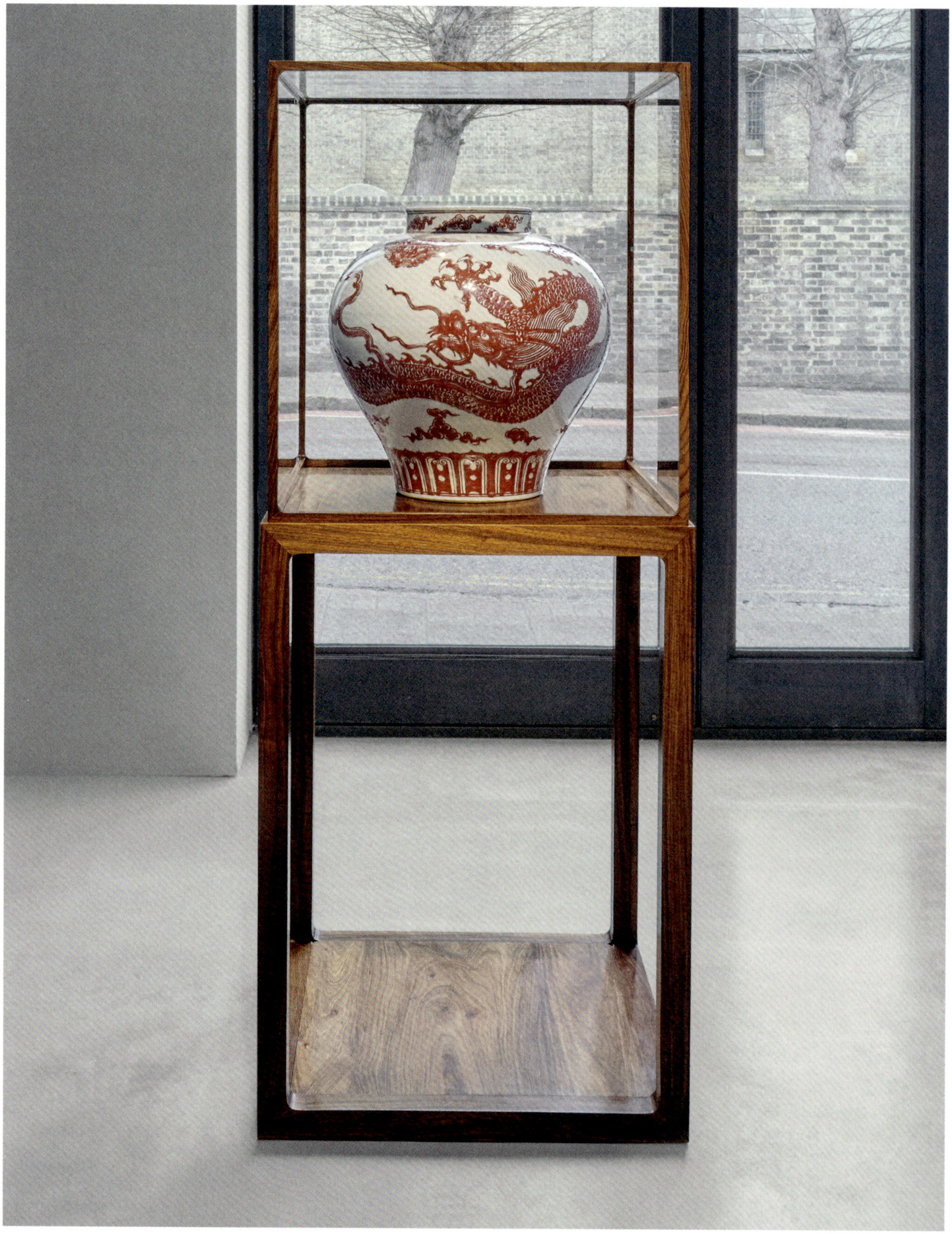

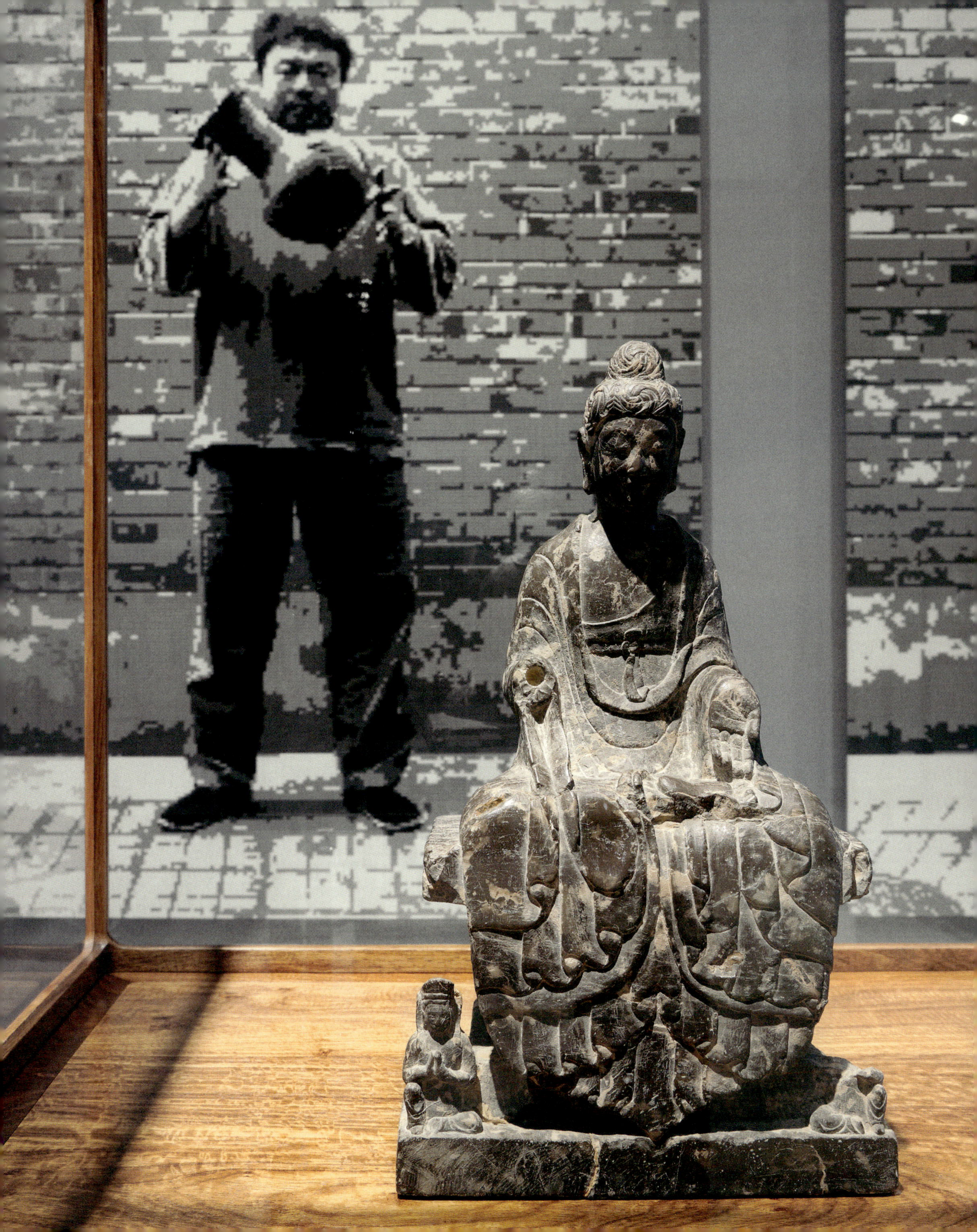

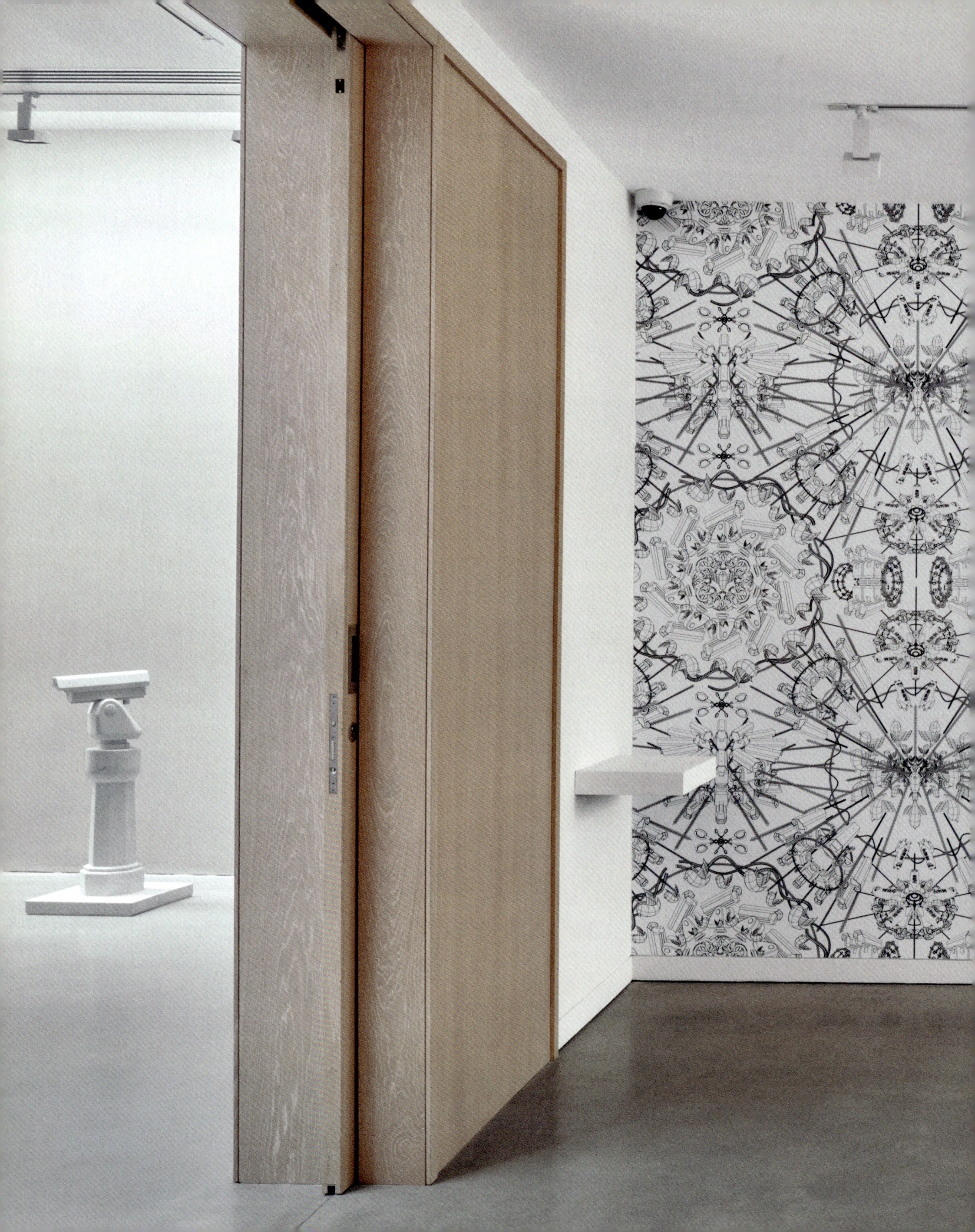

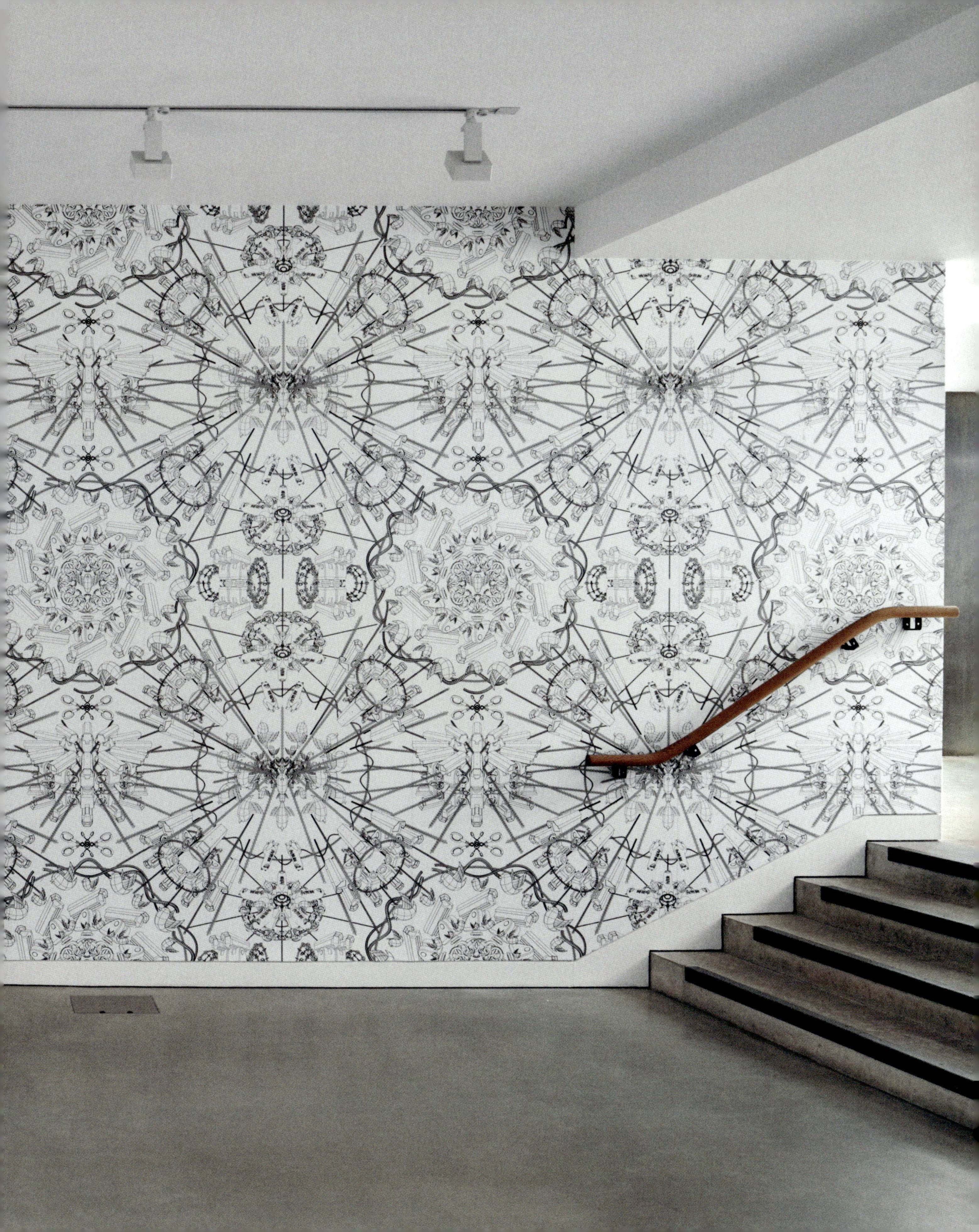

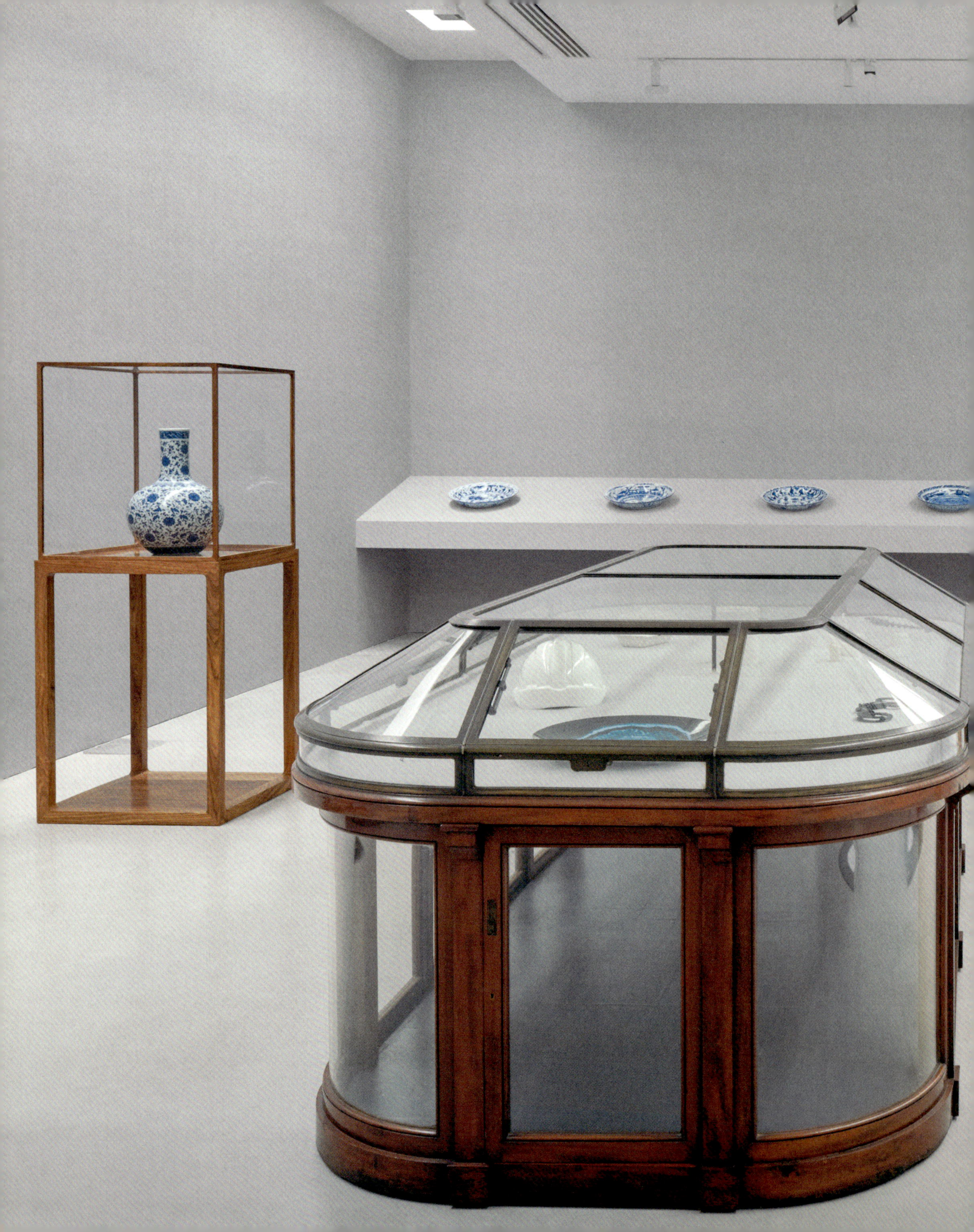

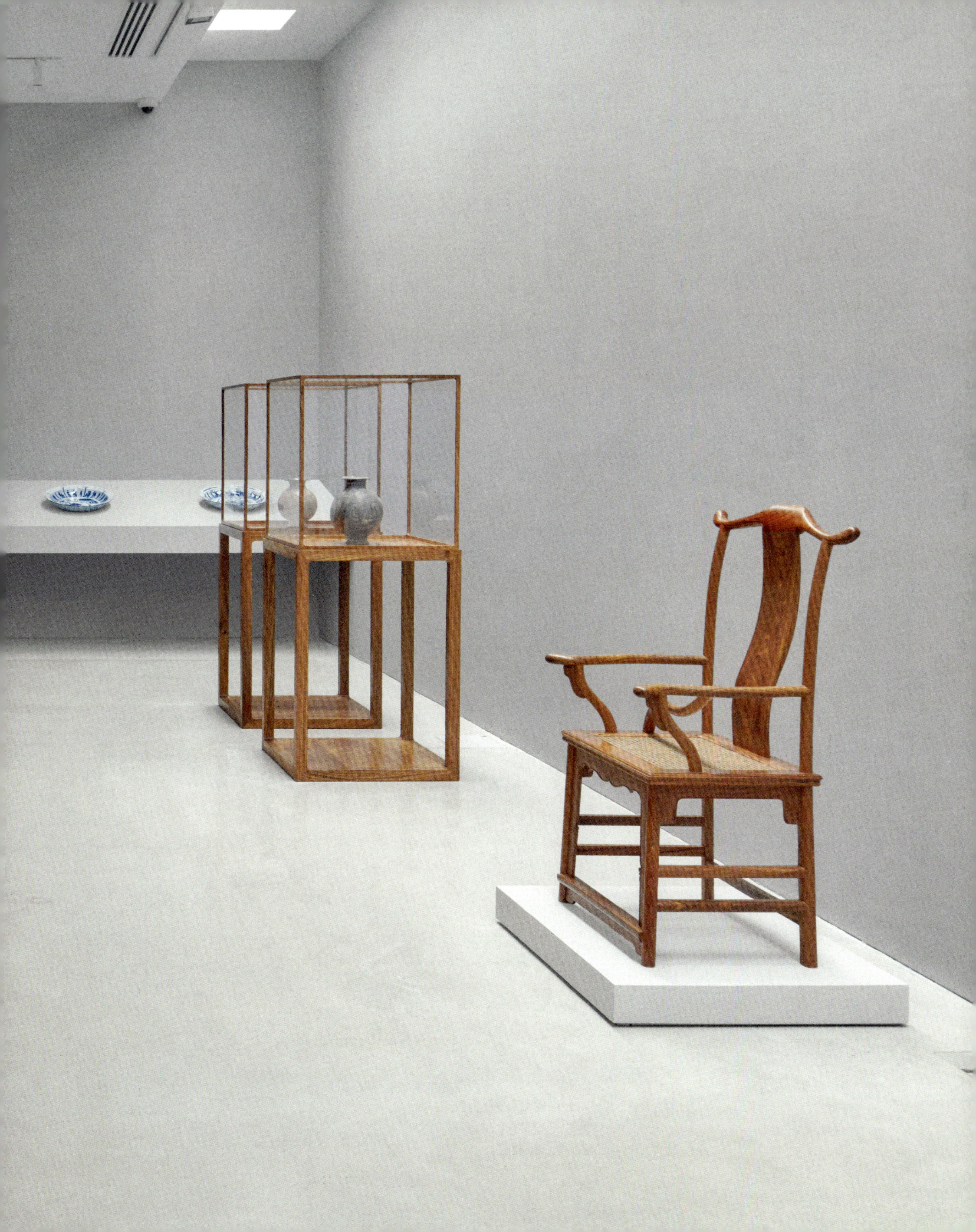

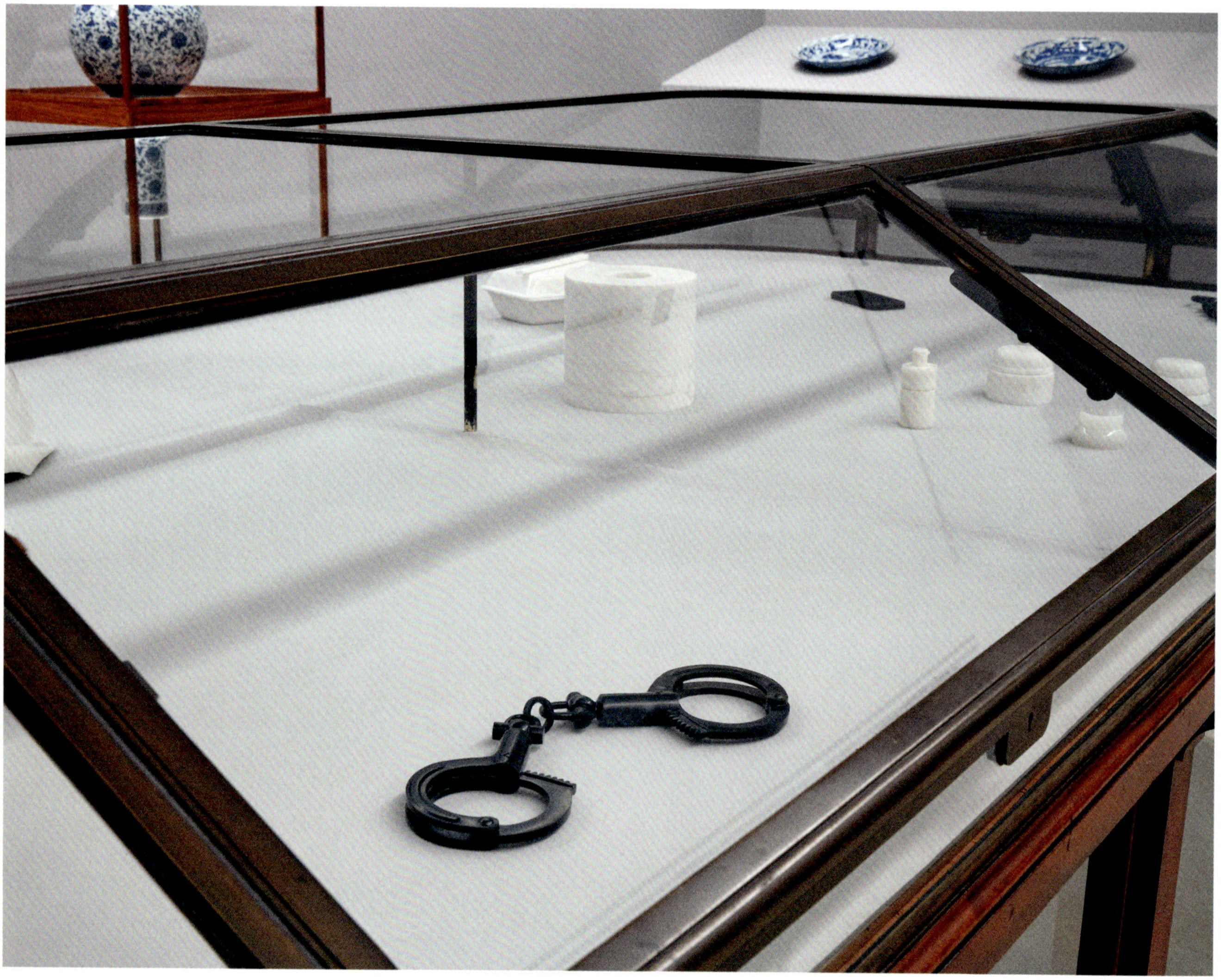

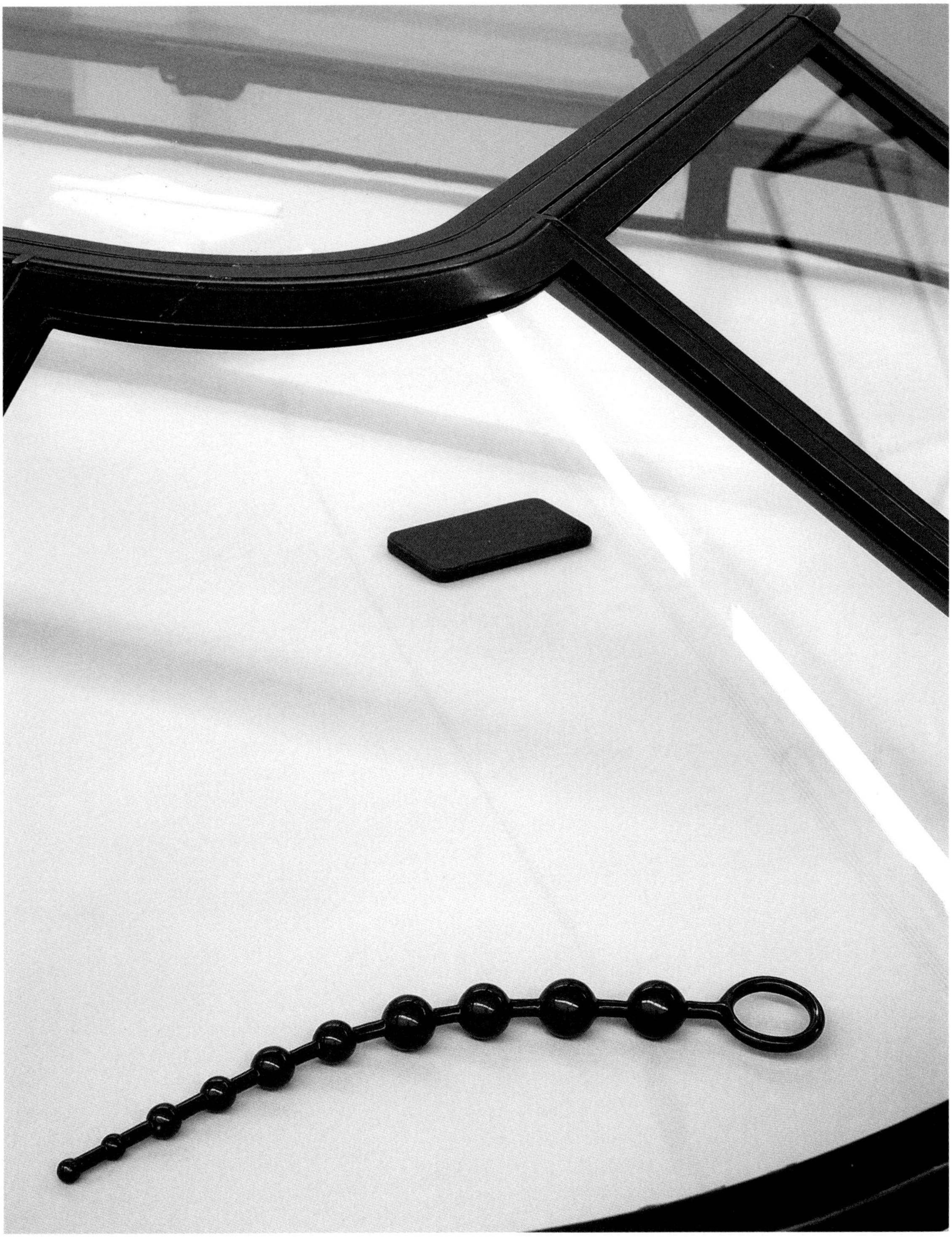

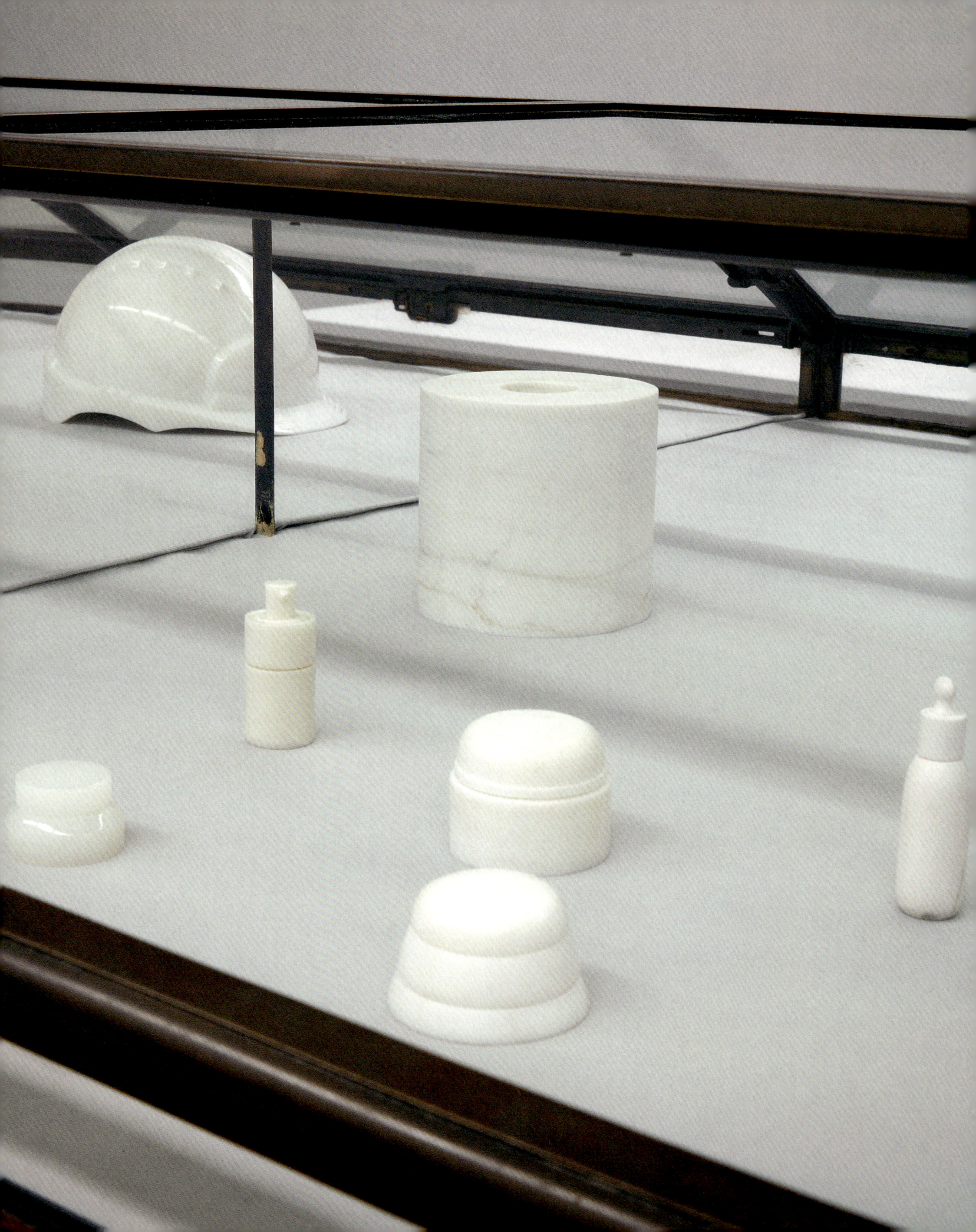

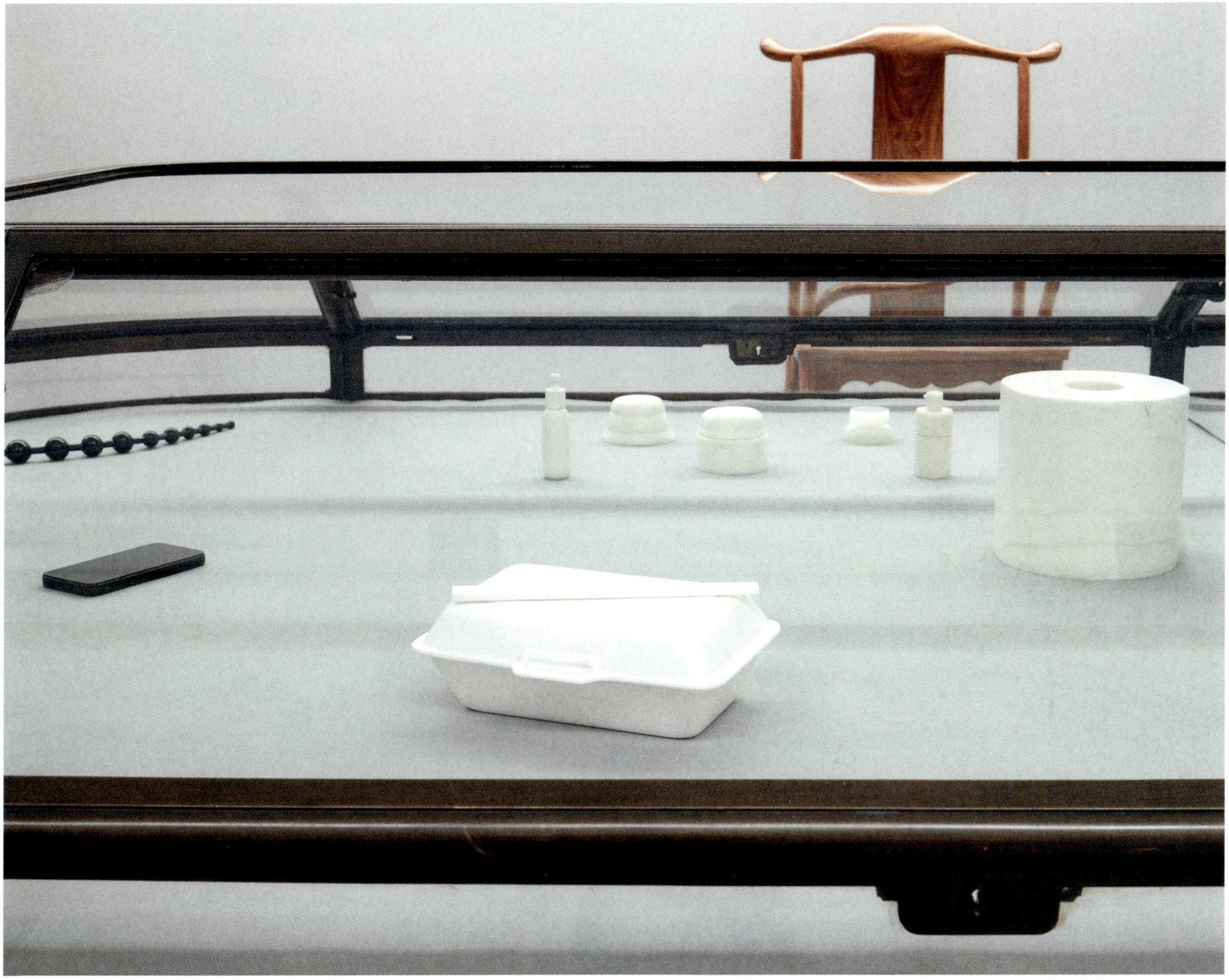

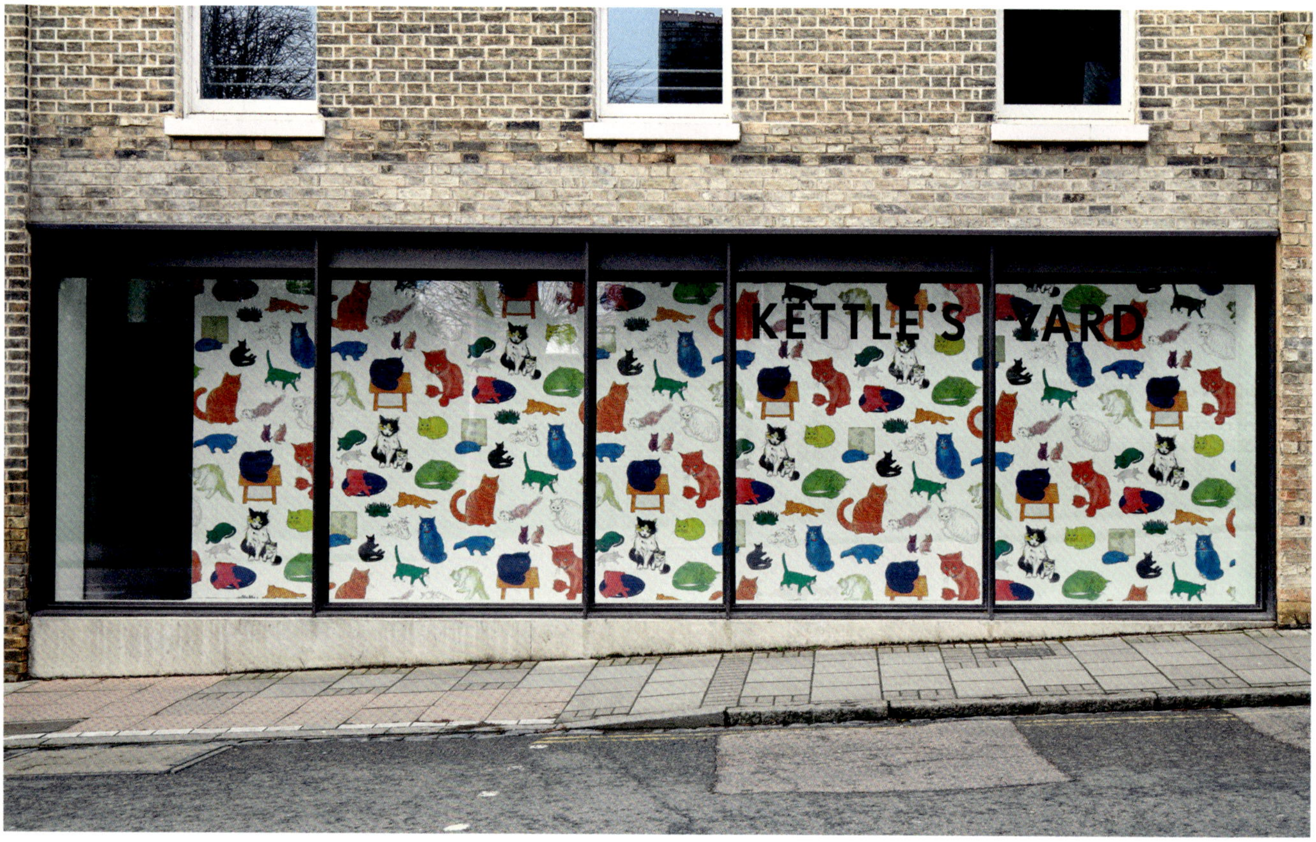
KETTLE'S YARD

AI WEIWEI
IN CONVERSATION

WITH
ELIZABETH BROWN
& ANDREW NAIRNE

EB/AN

Let's start with the title of your exhibition at Kettle's Yard, *The Liberty of Doubt*. You used this phrase in an interview in December 2020 in which you were discussing the lack of transparency in China in relation to the Covid-19 pandemic. What does this idea mean to you right now for how we appreciate art and understand current geopolitical issues?

AI WEIWEI

Human development and civilisation signal human beings' strong ability and spirit to doubt. This ability and spirit to doubt have permeated the history of human thoughts and political struggle. A certain ideal and new self-understanding is proposed for each era, which is directly and consistently related to regenerated doubt of oneself and former attestations. In the field of art, it is the same, especially for the development of contemporary art, which is established on the understanding of new things. The term 'new' refers to continuously breaking through and breaking free from the shackles of the old way of thinking. Liberty of doubt is thus a prerequisite for cultural and ideological development. Without this spirit, and as happened in some historical eras, it would be like a pool of stagnant water, from which corruption would emerge.

EB/AN

What was your motive in purchasing the 'historic' Chinese sculptures from an auction in Cambridge and including 14 of them in *The Liberty of Doubt*? Do you consider them readymade objects in the tradition of Marcel Duchamp?

AI WEIWEI

In my art practice, I have been influenced by Duchamp to a great extent. Duchamp's artworks, his readymades *Fountain* or *Bicycle Wheel*, for example, have been concerned with the way we form a judgement. When an object's function is eliminated, its new value can surface. In the same vein, political prerequisites, Chinese sociopolitics or the European refugee crisis are my readymade research topics.

At Kettle's Yard, historic Chinese sculptures as well as some that copy ancient Chinese traditions, commonly called counterfeits, purchased from an auction house in Cambridge, are incorporated within the subject matter of the exhibition. The discussion that it lays out surrounds the issues of real and fake, value, fact, judgement, and the origin and dissemination of culture. These are very basic yet profound questions to foreground and discuss.

EB/AN

You have identified five of the historic sculptures on display as 'fake' and nine as 'original' or 'real'. None of the pieces have been through a formal authentication process involving a range of experts. Of your works in the exhibition, two are perfectly made copies, 'fakes' based on highly valuable original porcelain vases. You have a long-standing interest in disrupting and questioning accepted notions of value and the distinctions that matter to museums and collectors. What do you hope visitors will consider in encountering your installation in the two galleries at Kettle's Yard?

AI WEIWEI

Cultural activities are very complex. The most important attribute of cultural activity is that there is no set standard. Sets of standards in culture, exhibitions or theories have been adhered to in certain periods of time; when there are set standards, all the complexity is lost. My artworks are more concerned with subversion, which I do not consider as destruction. Rather, it is a different way to look at the original value and to use it. Under this subversion we can see what cultural heritage is, how meaningful it is for us, and whether it is meaningful at all. These questions are formed during a happening, in the process of production, and along with people's reconsidered judgement; they are not intrinsic. This is what I have been interested in – that is, that there are no intrinsic standards in culture. In all standards there is always some prejudice or reflections originating from a certain value system, which cannot encompass other forms of aesthetics or ethics.

EB/AN

You have spoken about the English word 'fake' and its Chinese transliteration, a homonym for the English word 'fuck'. Your studio seal reads 'Fake Studio' – it marks the opening and closing pages of this catalogue. It recalls the subversive playing with language by dissidents in China to evade online censorship. Why is the idea of the fake – linguistically and conceptually – important?

AI WEIWEI

'Fake' is my definition for my own studio. In Chinese it is pronounced as *fa-ke* and has a different meaning. These are homographs that have two meanings in two different language systems. I am interested in multiple uses of one term, the misunderstanding that arises, and puns, which are also what Duchamp was interested in. We are birds of a feather. When an artist studio that creates real artistic value calls itself 'Fake Studio', is what it does still valuable? Or, when you call it 'fake', is it still a fake? These questions are very interesting to me.

EB/AN

A work like *Marble Toilet Roll* is an immediate emblem of the pandemic, while the sheer scale of the urgent unfolding health crisis in Wuhan is captured as though in real time in *Coronation*. Could you speak about the differences and notable contrast in scale between your small objects, your larger pieces and the cinematic scale of your documentary works?

AI WEIWEI

Thank you for asking this question. During the pandemic I created several artworks. One of them is *Coronation*, in which I talk about the origin of Covid-19 in Wuhan, China, about ordinary people's living conditions, and hospitals, which represent scientific and governmental institutions. I wanted to reflect upon the pandemic and issues in contemporary Chinese society. At the time of shooting the film, I was in Cambridge with my son and partner. There was not much we could do. There was no one on campus. We often went for walks, and during one of our walks I picked up a piece of wood. We took it back home and used kitchen knives to create something simple, in the shape of a toilet paper roll, together with my son. I wanted to show him how to complete an artwork. Afterwards we painted it in white and placed it in the toilet. It looked exactly like a real roll of toilet paper.

When I first went to the West, my strongest feeling, as someone coming from China, was that the toilet paper was so good and plentiful. I did not experience it in my childhood and not even until I was 20 years old. In the rural area where we lived, my father was assigned to cleaning toilets. There was not one single toilet paper roll in the toilet. Instead, there was cotton, rocks, plant leaves, clods. We never used toilet paper. When I arrived in the West, what struck me the most was that such nice paper would be used for toilets. Not even paper which we wrote on looked so pretty. Having lived in the US for many years and having got used to life in Europe for a while, when the pandemic started I was flabbergasted to see in the news that toilet paper was sold out everywhere in supermarkets. People would buy up the most unnoticeable and insignificant things out of fear; they were worried that daily necessities would run out. Public panic is not necessarily caused by a volcanic eruption or an earthquake, it could be triggered by one simple object. It is a real picture of the psychology, spiritual condition and human condition of our time. I felt that it would be a very important object to memorialise our era, so I created it. It is just like my large-scale films, but from a different perspective and in a humorous way.

EB/AN

Visitors to the exhibition will be able to see artworks in many different materials, usually handmade and always beautifully crafted or produced. Can you tell us about your interest in materials, from jade to LEGO?

AI WEIWEI

In ancient times, artists were understood as artisans who had skills in craft. I have been personally interested in craftsmanship because it shows how people think and the kind of language they use to think. Be it jade sculpture or other crafts, craftsmanship has its own complete language which has been there for thousands of years in China. Ceramics in China reached the highest level of expression. The same goes for LEGO today. To different degrees they reflect an era's standard of living and how people use different languages as carriers of emotions and thoughts.

Since 2000, LEGO has been my favourite medium. I will continue to use the medium of LEGO to express the situation today, which is both complicated and plain, serious and humorous.

EB/AN

Your secret imprisonment in China, referenced in works like *Handcuffs*, has been matched by the authorities attempting to 'disappear' your online presence – references to you have been systematically erased on Weibo, whether they support or criticise your work. Meanwhile, you have used blogging and social media as 'drawing', as you put it in one of your conversations with Hans Ulrich Obrist. This is alluded to in *The Animal that Looks Like a Llama But is Really an Alpaca* – one of the wallpapers included in the Kettle's Yard exhibition, where we see the Twitter bluebird logo surrounded by handcuffs. How has your use of the Internet as a medium evolved over the last few years, and in the light of the pandemic?

AI WEIWEI

The Internet has accompanied my artistic journey over the past 15 years or more. I have been exhibiting my artworks and surfing the Internet for the same amount of time, but I spend far more time on the Internet than producing artworks. There was a period of time when I was on the Internet 24/7. Being able to express myself directly through language on the Internet is very attractive to me, as well as the speed of communication and sensitivity. After leaving China, however, things have changed a lot for me. In the West the Internet is basically open, and the related social issues and human interactions are very different, so I have become a lot less interested. Today I just use some basic platforms such as Twitter and Instagram to receive information and express myself. I have no necessity of using the Internet; the necessity doesn't exist for me anymore.

EB/AN

On a different note: another of your wallpapers includes a drawing of two of your cats, made with your son, Ai Lao. Like Andy Warhol, your cats are often found in your work and conversations. We couldn't finish this interview without asking you to tell us what it is you love about cats.

AI WEIWEI

After we arrived in Cambridge, we moved once so that my son Ai Lao could keep pets. I have always thought that human beings are very lucky to have the company of these animals. It makes us feel less lonely. These animals are independent and very tolerant and forgiving towards us human beings. The earth should be a world of animals, and they allow us to coexist with them. In reality, people are harming animals much more now than in any period in human history. Many animals are facing extinction. It is a miserable situation.

I like cats very much because of their independent character, alertness and understanding of human beings; I have feelings approximating reverence for them. Cats have been regarded as psychic animals since ancient times, whether in China or ancient Greece. What's even more interesting is that if a selfie of mine would be seen by 100 people, a cat photo would be seen by 1,000 people. I believe that everyone can share this happiness.

CATALOGUE

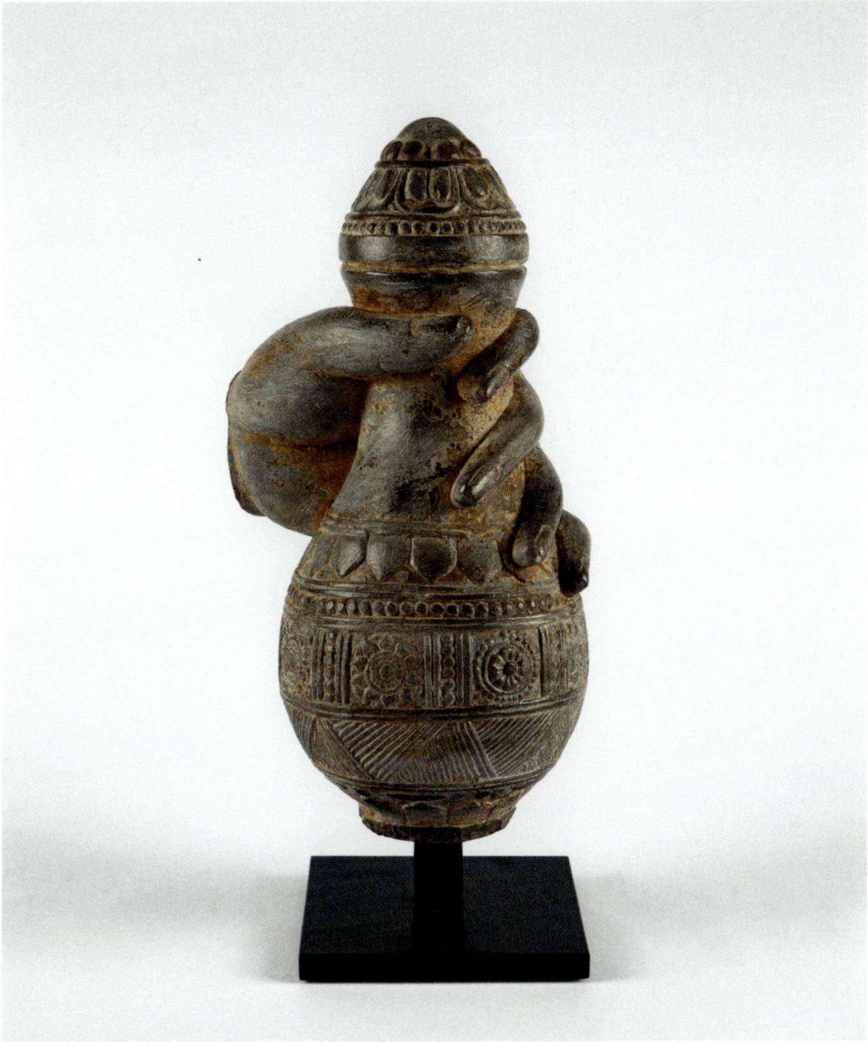

A Chinese lacquered greystone
fragmentary hand clutching a vase
Stone, height: 23.5 cm, in Northern Qi dynasty style

This stone hand with fingers curled around a bottle may have belonged to the bodhisattva Avalokiteshvara, shown clasping an ornately decorated bottle used for holding pure water. The bottle still retains some of the lacquer pigment that once decorated the entire sculpture. Avalokiteshvara, venerated for his kindness, compassion, mercy and love, is typically shown holding a bottle in the left hand and a willow branch in the right as he sprinkles the divine nectar of life. The ornate bottle, with bands of pearl beadings and cabochons, suggests that the figure itself would have been elaborately jewelled, a design element that became standard in Chinese Buddhist art from the second half of the sixth century. HE

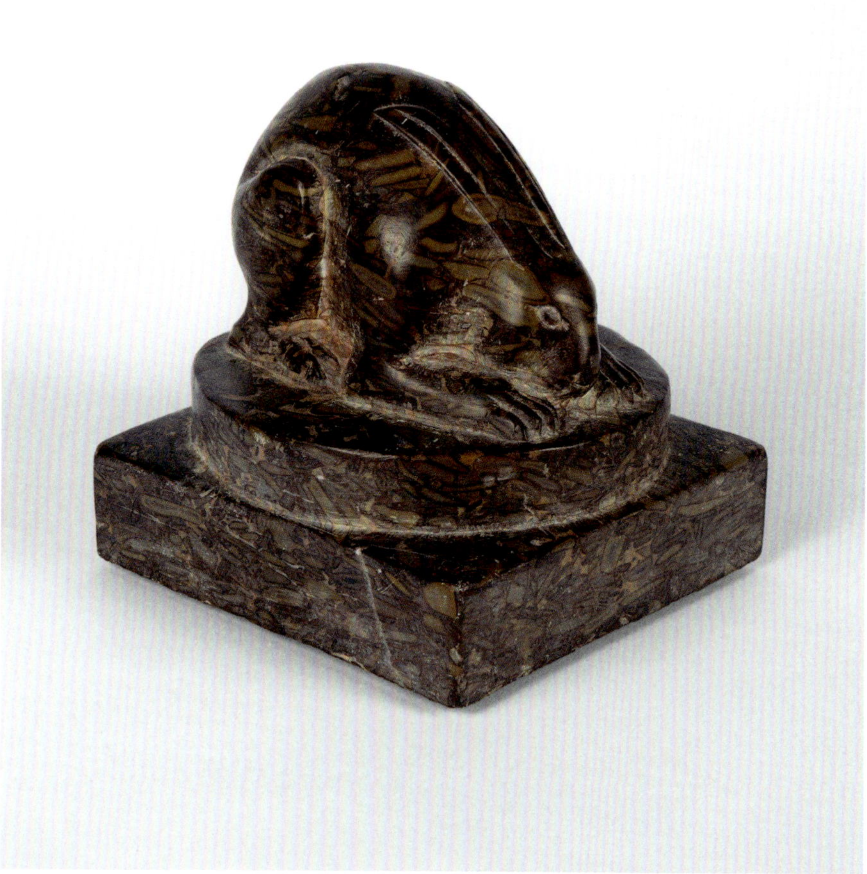

A Chinese red puddingstone crouched hare
Stone, height: 13 cm, in Sui dynasty style

Carved in the rare puddingstone and modelled in a naturalistic style, this figure of a crouching hare displays the artisan's mastery of the material and subject matter. In China, the hare is among the most propitious animals, closely associated with Daoism and the wish for longevity. It is often depicted in the company of the moon goddess, making the elixir of immortality by pounding herbs with a mortar and pestle. It is the fourth animal in the Chinese zodiac and symbolises compassion, productivity and reproduction. How this carving functioned is unclear, but objects of this type were often used as paperweights placed in the studios of the scholar-literati. Apart from its utilitarian function, it was also an object of inspiration, bringing to mind the hare's Daoist associations. HE

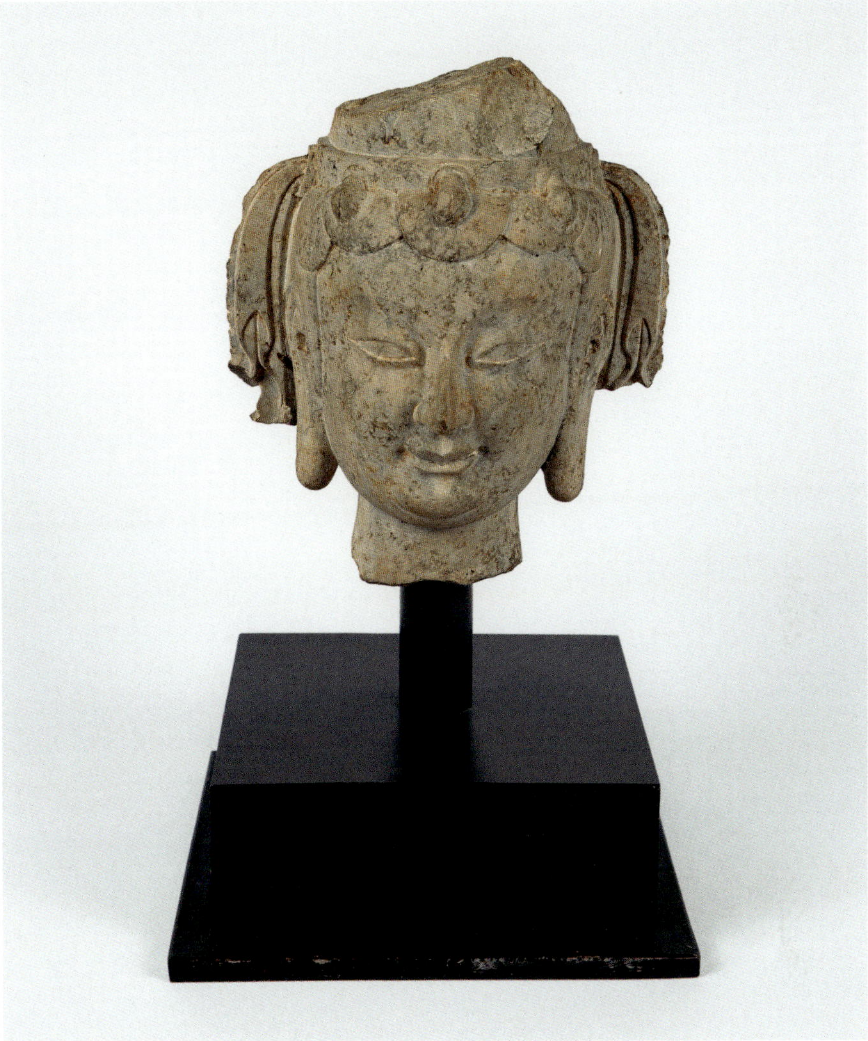

A Chinese pale stone head fragment of a bodhisattva
Stone, height: 18.5 cm, perhaps Sui dynasty

Depicted with delicate facial features and bearing a gentle, benign smile, this fragment of a bodhisattva figure displays characteristics of early Buddhist sculptural tradition. The figure has a finely carved face representing a youthful, almost feminine appearance of a bodhisattva, a being who has attained enlightenment but who, motivated by his compassion for mankind, decides to postpone personal salvation until all sentient beings are saved and enlightened. The figure's continued engagement with the world is represented by his hairstyle, which is combed into fine strands, lying in loops on the forehead and falling to the shoulders on the sides, where they are held by lotus bud-shaped clasps. This rich imagery symbolises the material world where the bodhisattva resides. HE

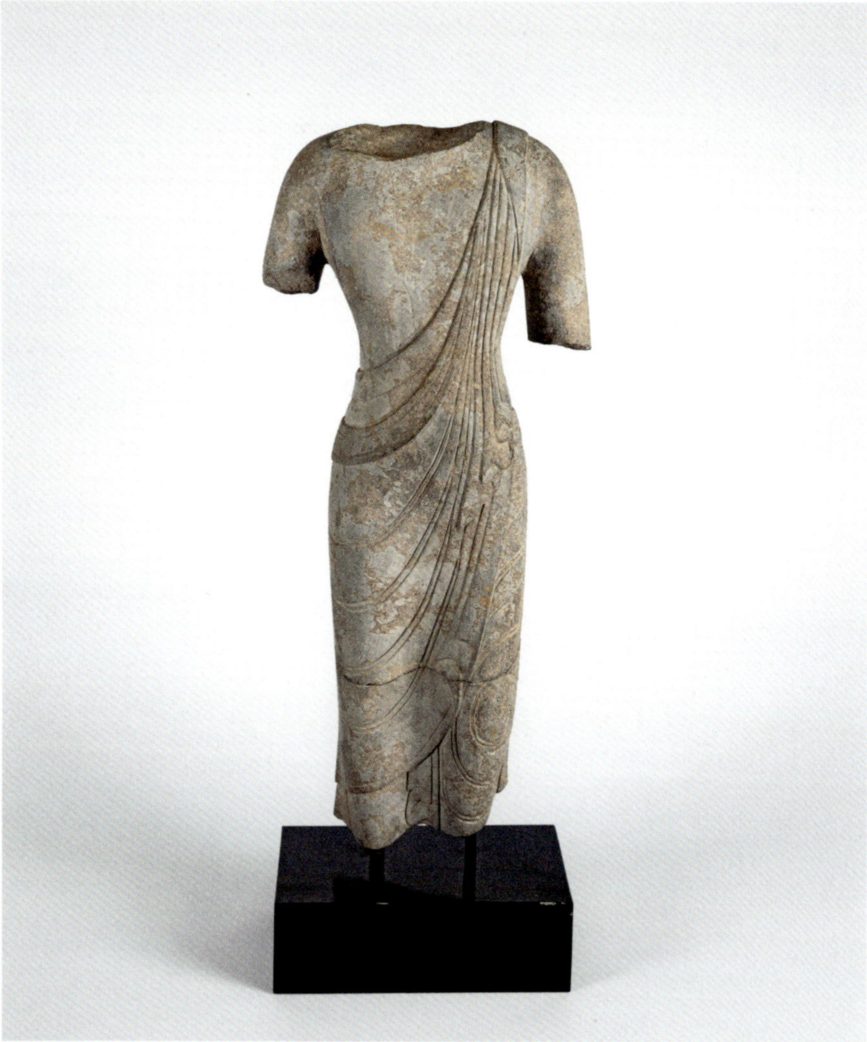

A Chinese limestone fragmentary torso of a Buddha
Stone, height: 41 cm, in Wei dynasty style

This fragmentary figure of a standing Buddha reflects an artistic style that remains somewhat restrained in the treatment of the body but nevertheless shows signs of distinct three-dimensionality. This is evident in the depiction of the figure's slender waist with the right knee ever so slightly bent forward. The Buddha is wearing a monk's robe that falls in pleats and folds, giving a sense of the fabric's sumptuous nature. The missing right arm would have been raised in *abhaya* mudra, the gesture of protection, with the left hand lowered in *varada* mudra, signifying Buddha's great charity and compassion. HE

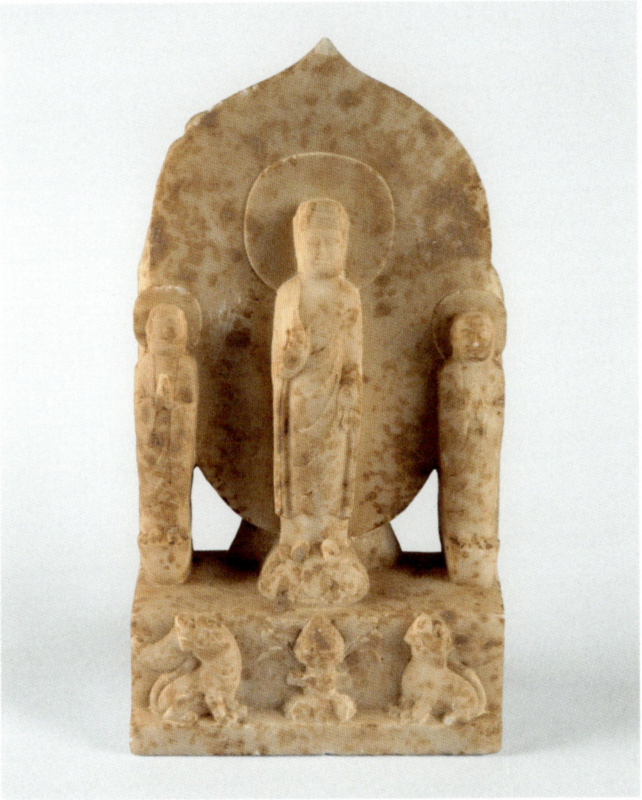

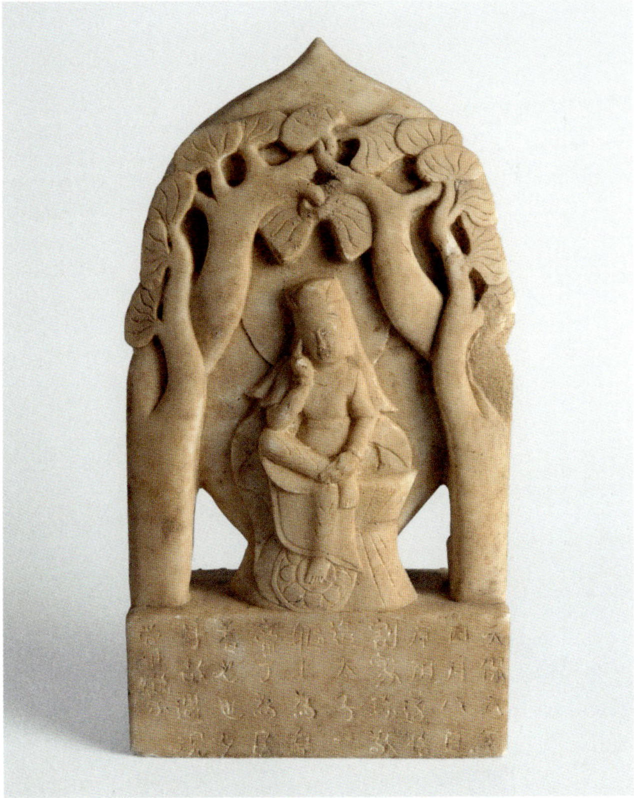

A Chinese white marble Buddhist triad stela with aureole
Stone, height: 23 cm, in Northern Qi dynasty style

The figure of Shakyamuni Buddha, standing in the centre of a rectangular plinth carved in high relief with a pair of seated lions confronting an incense burner framed by lotus petals, is flanked by his disciples Ananda and Kasyapa. The two monks, clad in long monastic robes with light folds, bear a serene expression and press their hands together in the prayer of *anjali* mudra. The figures all stand against a large flame-form aureole or *mandorla* which is left undecorated, although it may have been painted in a vibrant gold colour originally. The reverse of the stela is carved with the figure of Buddha seated under the Bodhi Fig Tree where he meditated and ultimately achieved enlightenment. The plinth is inscribed with a dedication suggesting that the stela was made as a commission for private or family worship. HE

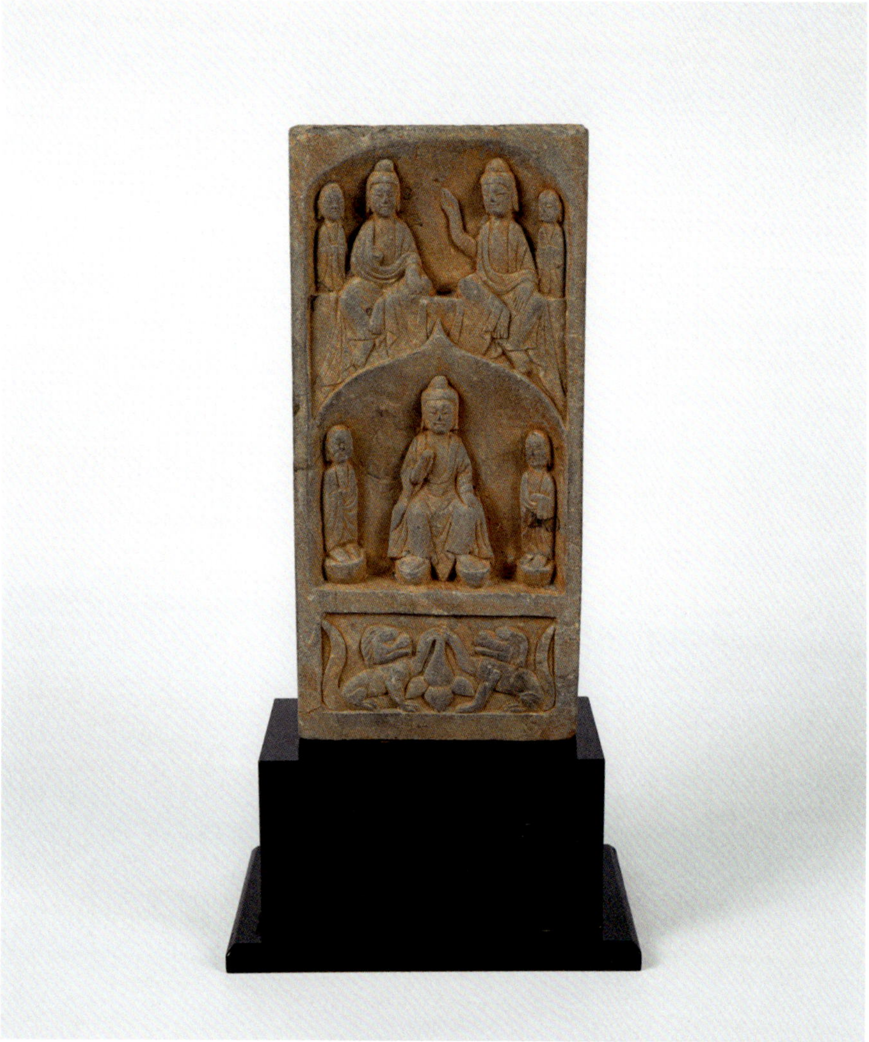

A Chinese limestone Buddhist votive stela
Stone, height: 30 cm, in Northern Wei dynasty style

Rectangular Buddhist stone tablets known as votive stelae, carved on all four sides with figures of the Buddha, monks, bodhisattvas and images of donors, were popular devotional objects, commissioned by pious individuals and families and erected in temple courtyards, public spaces or even at major crossroads. By commissioning such objects, devotees hoped to gain spiritual benefits for themselves and their families. Along with images, stelae sometimes also contain carved inscriptions with a date and the donors' names. Iconographically they can be complex, as seen here, with each register showing different niches, with the main Shakyamuni Buddha in the centre, flanked by his devoted disciples, the two monks Ananda and Kasyapa. HE

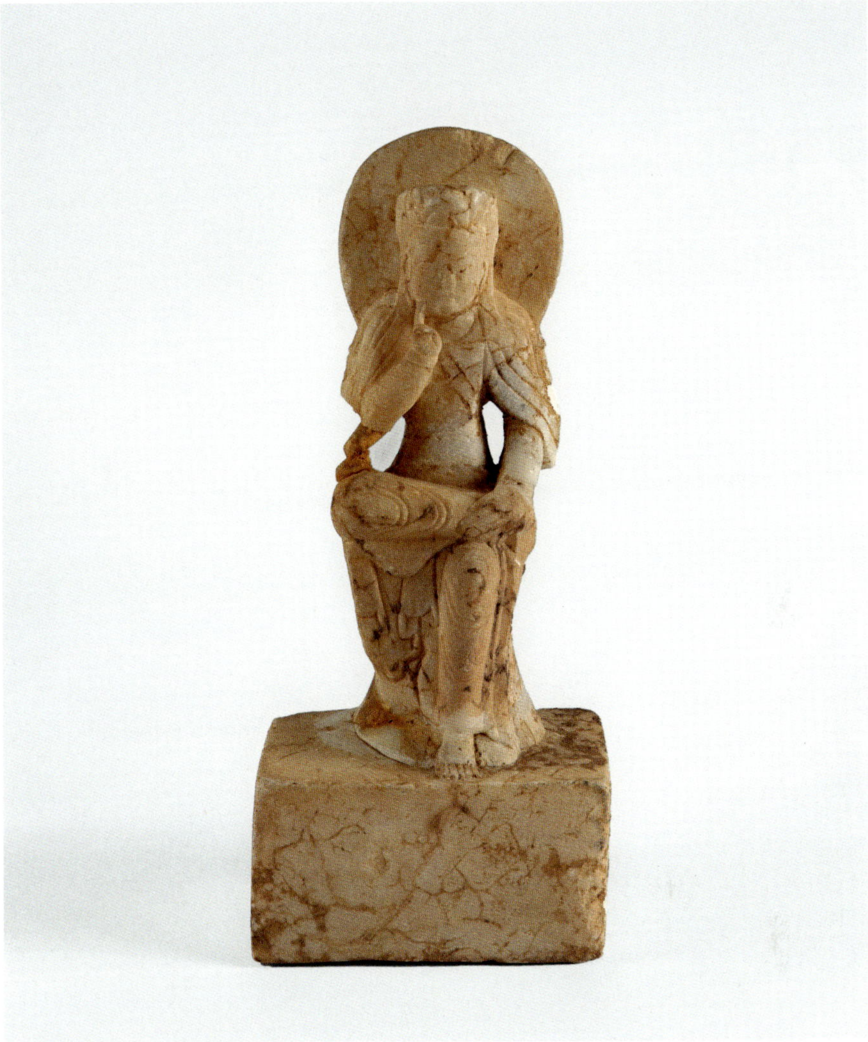

A Chinese white marble figure of Maitreya Buddha
Stone, height: 23.5 cm, in Northern Qi dynasty style

Carved in white marble, this figure of a bodhisattva represents the Maitreya Buddha, the future Buddha of this world. In Buddhist tradition, Maitreya is a bodhisattva who resides in Heaven and descends to preach the *dharma* (law) when the teachings of Siddhartha Gautama, the historical Buddha, have completely decayed. The figure here is shown seated in a contemplative pose on a high plinth, with left hand resting on the right foot, crossed over the left knee, while gently touching his cheek with his right finger. The pose itself is intended to evoke the moment of awakening, the time when Maitreya Buddha was still a prince, thus giving the sculpture an added layer of meaning. HE

A Chinese veined marble seated figure of Laozi
Stone, height: 58.5 cm, in Northern Wei dynasty style

The historical figure of Laozi, reputed author of the sixth-century BCE primary Daoist text the *Daode jing* (Classic of the Way and Virtue), is shown in this sculpture as the Highest Venerable Lord, primary deity of the Daoist pantheon. Wearing the long-sleeved belted robe associated with the Chinese scholar-official, Laozi is bearded with refined facial features, hair pulled up in a bun under a hat, elongated earlobes signifying his great wisdom and holding a fan-like object in his hand, a Daoist attribute denoting the wish for longevity. The influence of Buddhist iconography on this otherwise distinctly Daoist imagery is evident in the use of the lotus throne, usually reserved for Buddha, illustrating the mixing of Buddhist and Daoist elements in the arts of medieval China. HE

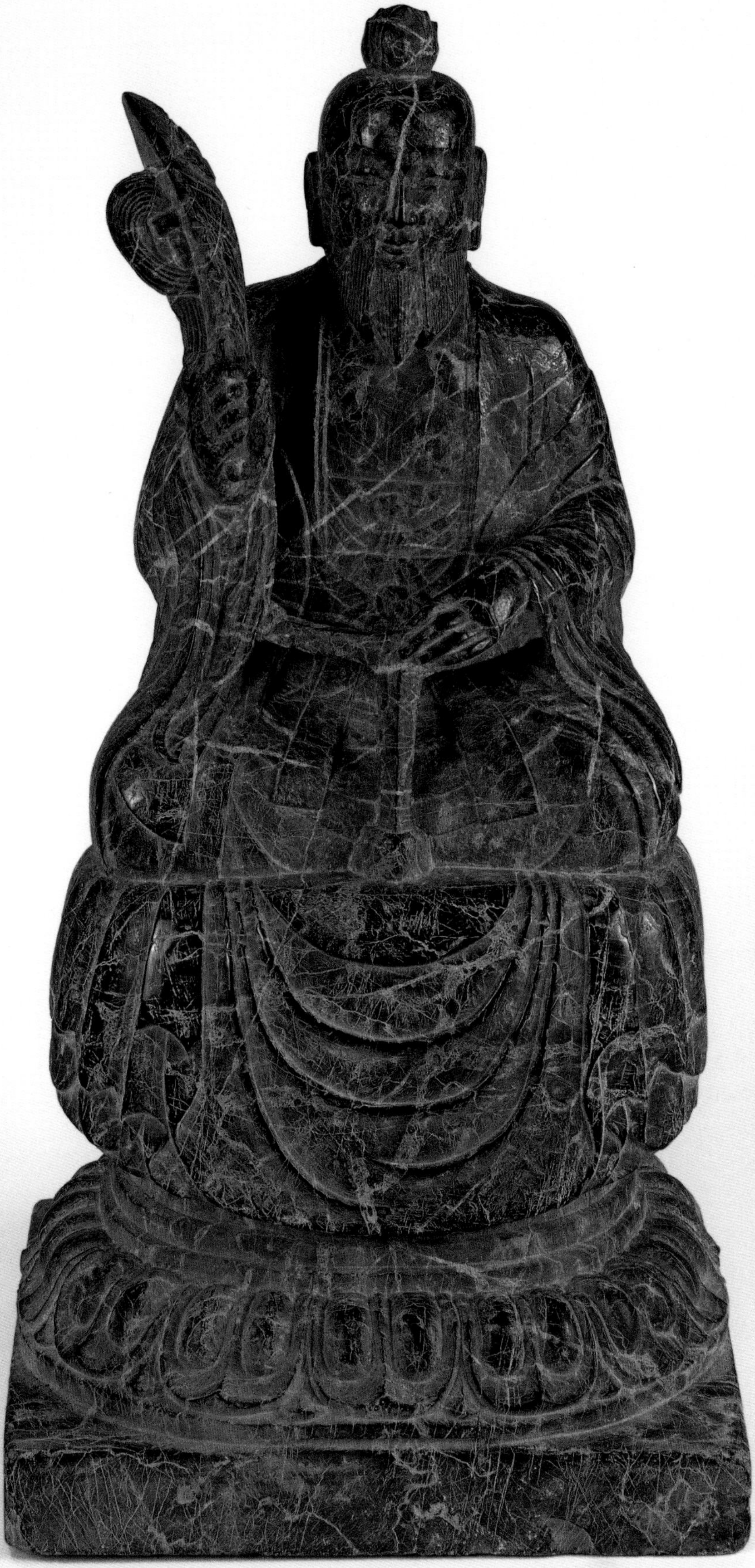

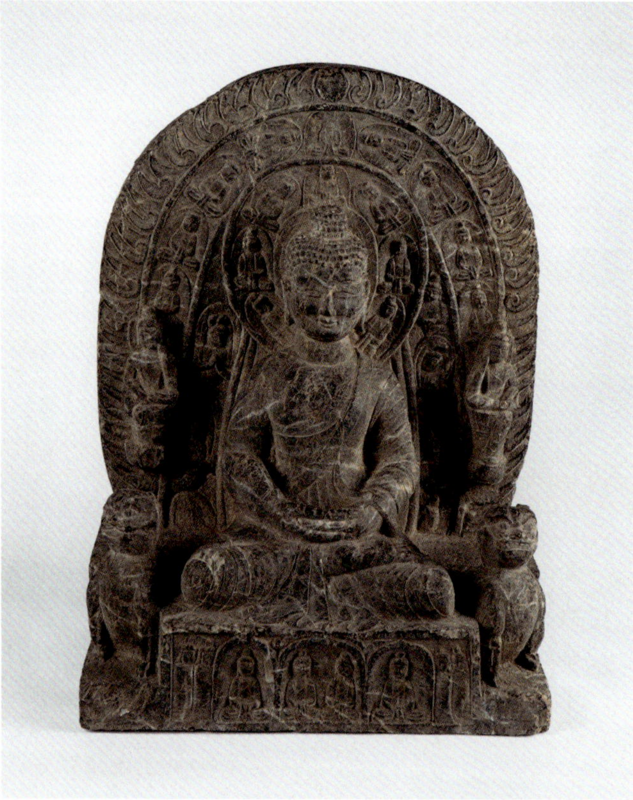

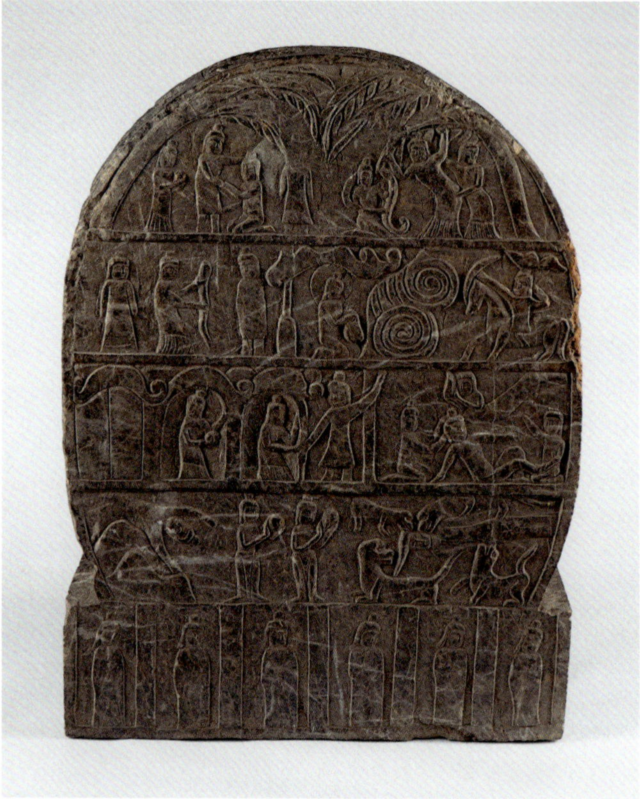

A Chinese grey-veined stone Buddhist triad group
Stone, height: 45 cm, in Northern Wei dynasty style

The central figure of Shakyamuni Buddha is depicted with his hands resting on his lap in the gesture of *dhyāna*, the mudra of meditation. Shakyamuni, the historical Buddha, attained enlightenment under the Bodhi Fig Tree while in deep contemplation. Seated on a throne flanked by two lions, symbols of royalty and leadership, in this triad sculpture he is attended by two bodhisattvas depicted in the pose of *rajalilasana*, or the 'royal ease'. Bodhisattvas are enlightened beings who choose to remain on earth to help mortals attain enlightenment. Buddhist triads of this type would have been placed in temples or family shrines for worship. HE

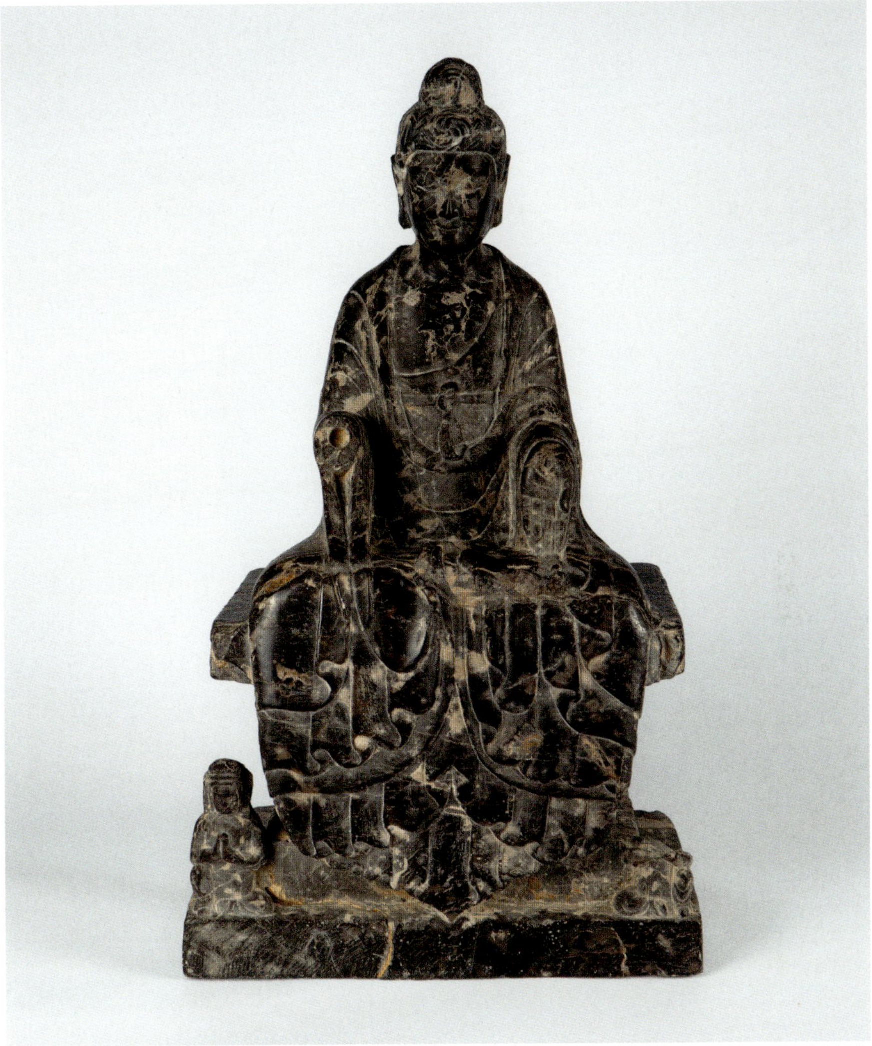

A Chinese mottled dark stone seated Buddhist deity
Stone, height: 38 cm, in Wei dynasty style

Seated on a throne flanked by two bodhisattvas, Buddha is shown with his right hand likely raised in *abhaya* mudra, signifying protection and the dispelling of fear, and the left hand in *varada* mudra, standing for charity and compassion. His hair is arranged in tight spiral curls over the *ushnīsha*, a top-knot that also symbolises his teachings of the *dharma*, the laws and principles that govern the universe. He is wearing a monk's robe, which falls in heavy symmetrical pleats and folds to the front. The two bodhisattvas accompanying him are depicted in *rajalilasana*, or the 'royal ease', a posture closely associated with deities and rulers in Buddhist iconography. HE

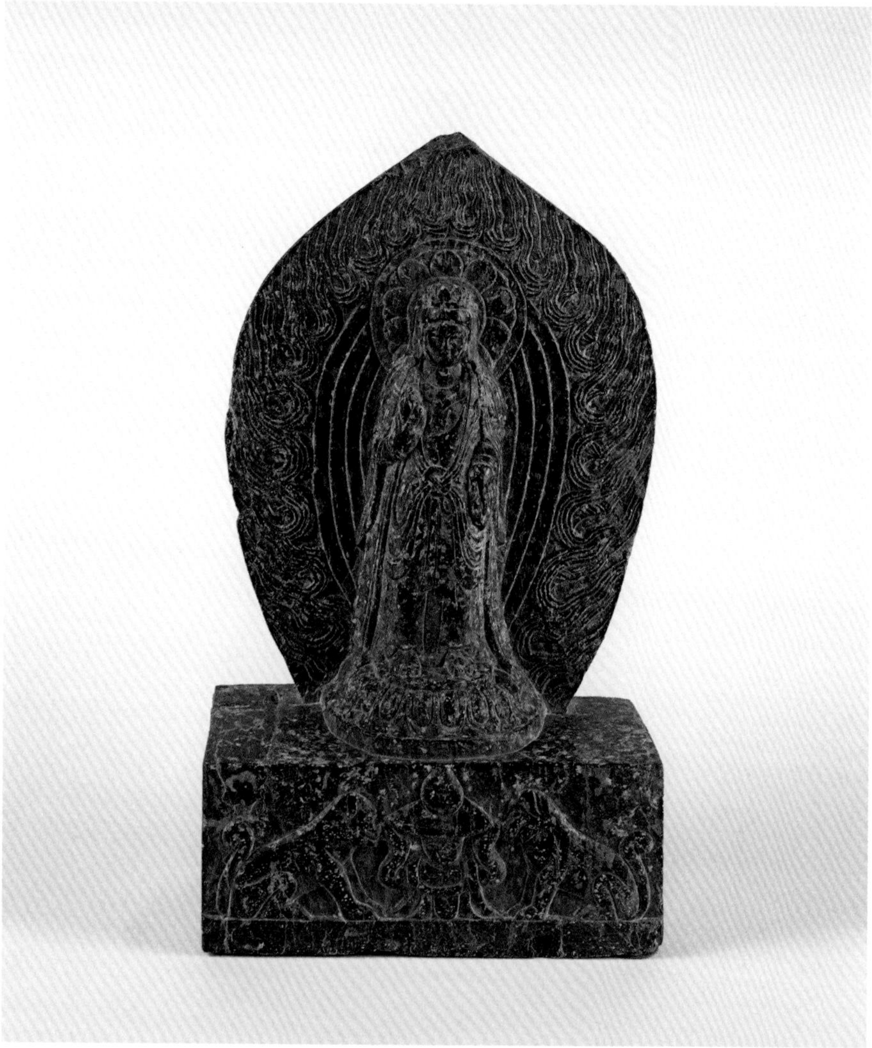

A Chinese carved stone standing figure
of Avalokiteshvara with aureole
Stone, height: 34 cm, in Wei dynasty style

On a lotus base, the figure of Avalokiteshvara, the bodhisattva of infinite compassion and mercy, stands in front of a large flame-form aureole or *mandorla*, signifying his godlike qualities and importance within the Buddhist pantheon. The rectangular plinth beneath him is decorated in high relief with an incense burner between two small confronting lions on the front face, a design element that became commonplace by the end of the fourth century and may be seen in many small Buddhist images in particular. Figural sculptures of this type were often made for personal devotion and served as portable shrines during travels or pilgrimage. HE

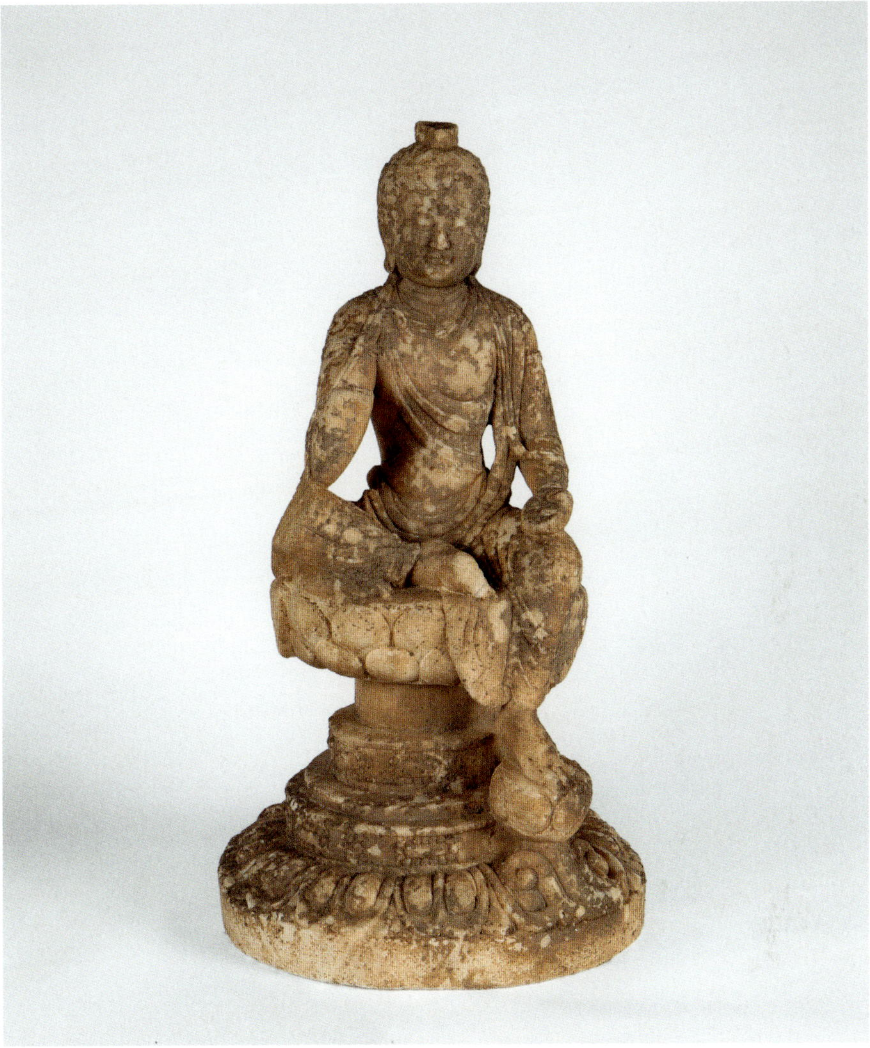

A Chinese white marble Buddhist
deity (figure of a Bodhisattva)
Stone, height: 42 cm, in Northern Wei dynasty style

This marble figure shows a bodhisattva seated in meditation on an ornately decorated lotus throne. Bodhisattvas are enlightened beings on the path towards Buddhahood but who delay entering nirvana in order to help others attain enlightenment. The face of this figure has delicately modelled features with downcast eyes and a gentle, almost invisible smile that indicates his spiritual equilibrium. The elaborately fashioned throne with its tiered layers and deeply carved decoration of pearl roundels is worth noting. The sculpture bears traces of pigment, suggestive of the fact that votive images of this type were originally painted in vibrant colours and would have served for personal veneration. HE

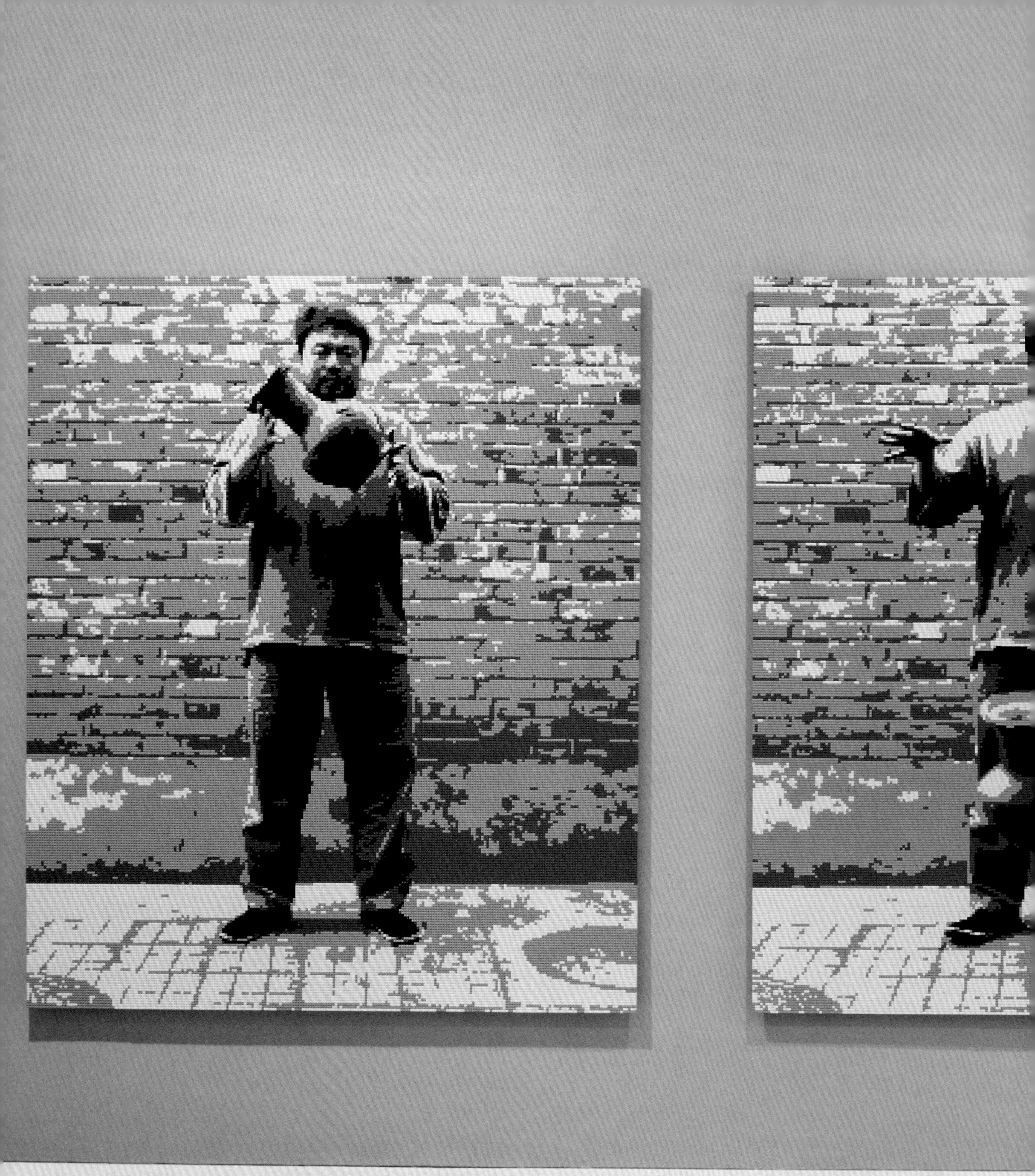

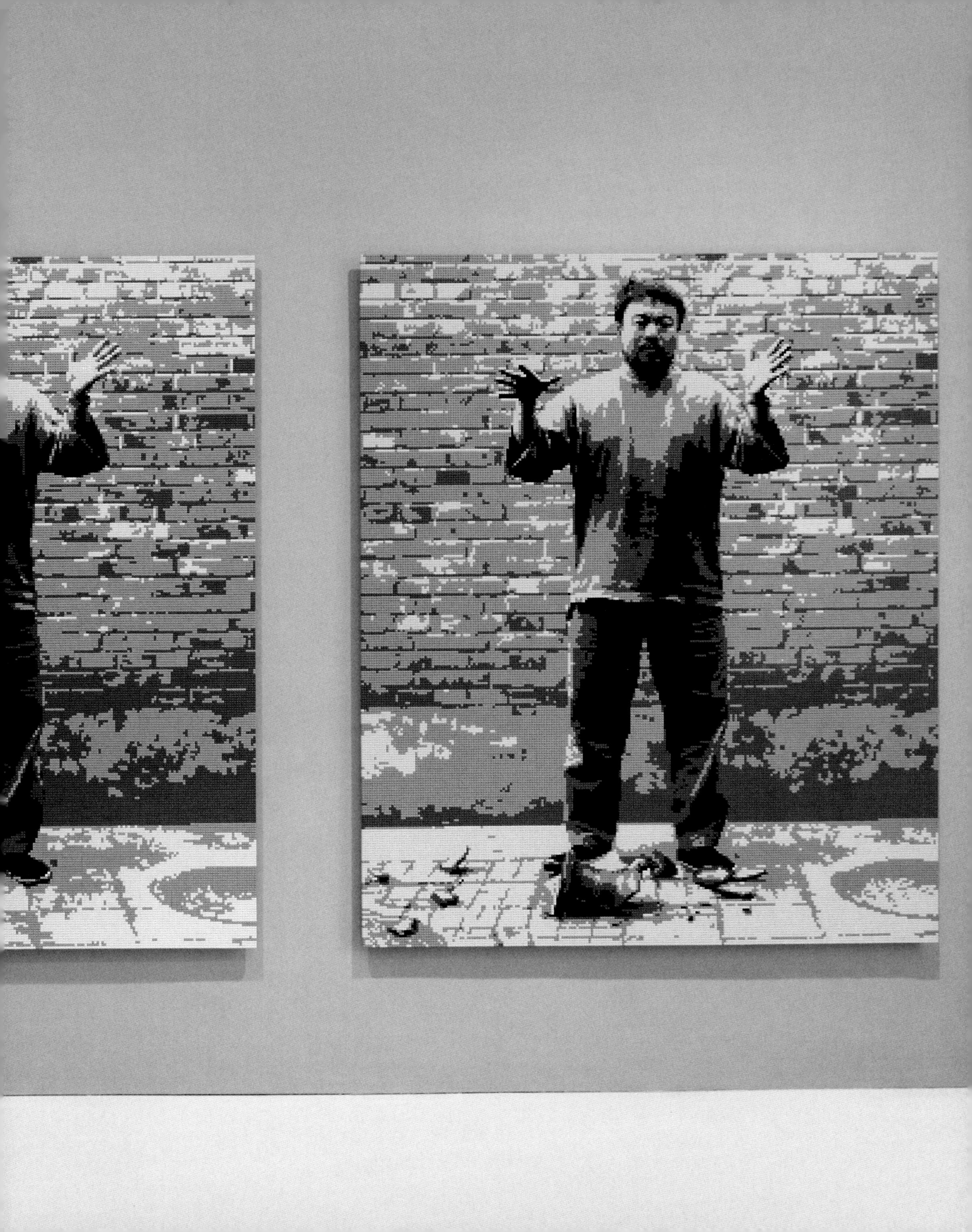

PREVIOUS PAGE

Dropping a Han Dynasty Urn, 2015
LEGO bricks, 230 × 192 × 3 cm each

In 1995, Ai Weiwei intentionally dropped a Han dynasty urn while being photographed – simultaneously destroying and making. His transformative act drew attention to the Chinese government's widespread destruction of the country's heritage. The action was originally captured in three photographs, and is here recreated in LEGO in an act of careful reconstruction, piece by piece. While centuries old, many thousands of these ancient urns have survived into the present day.

Dragon Vase, 2017
Porcelain, Ø 51 × 50 cm

The *Dragon Vase* is a near exact replica of a Ming period (1368–1644) vase bearing the motif of a dragon that sold for one of the highest recorded prices at auction. In Imperial times, only the emperor was allowed use of the five-clawed dragon in the making of images. Members of the Imperial court were allowed use of a four-clawed dragon. Improper use of the number of claws was punishable by death. Ai's reinterpretation of the Ming vase is only distinguishable through the subtle addition of a sixth claw.

In the Ming dynasty a blue-and-white glaze was often used, but a red glaze was more rare and precious, as the colour requires a more precise firing temperature.

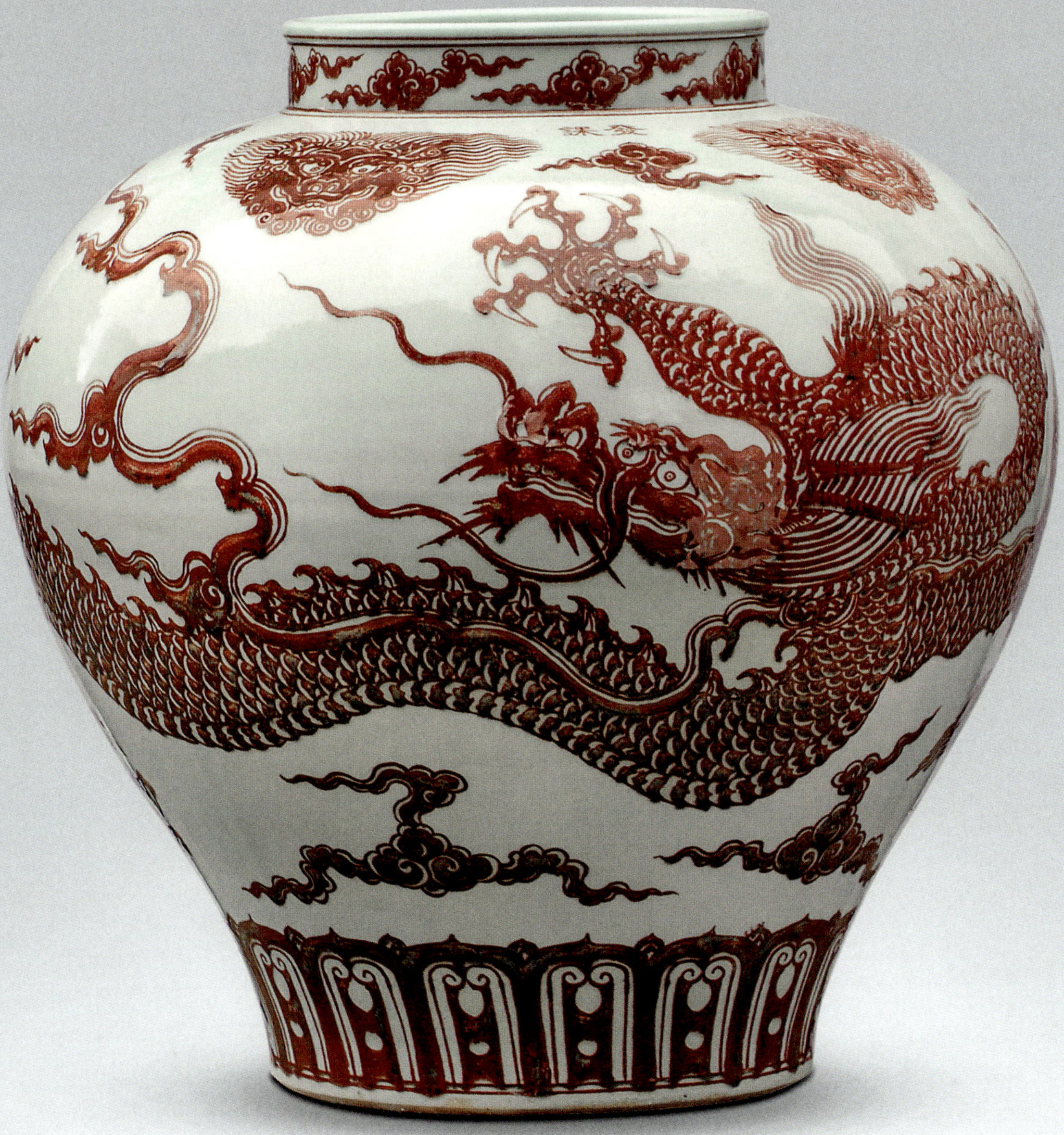

Vault-of-Heaven Vase, 1997
Porcelain, Ø 35 × 50 cm

This vase is a replica of a blue-and-white porcelain jar in the style of the Qing dynasty during the Kangxi reign (1661–1772). Modern imitations of these prized antiques have become prevalent in recent years. Rendered with minute attention to detail, they can only be identified as 'fakes' by radiocarbon dating. Ai's vase responds to questions of authenticity and value, whether aesthetic, cultural or monetary.

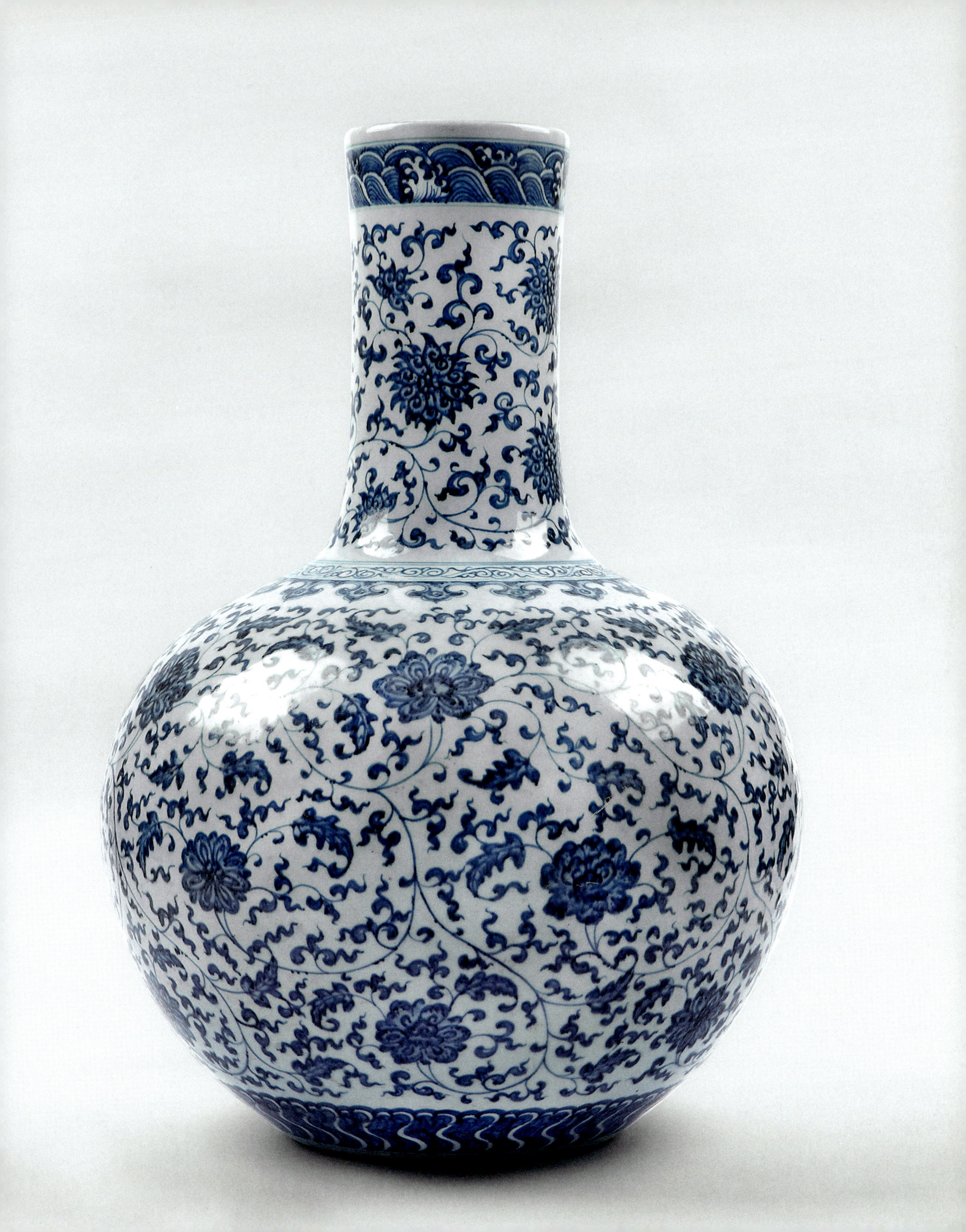

Blue-and-White Porcelain Plates, 2017
Porcelain, set of 6, Ø 48 × 8 cm each

Inspired by the ancient Greek epic the *Odyssey*, Ai reflects on the cyclical nature of history in the imagery of these plates. Ai draws a correlation between the journey undertaken by Odysseus, a king and soldier who embarks on a treacherous 10-year journey home after the Trojan War, and the ongoing global refugee crisis. The plates show six themes: War, Ruins, the Journey, Crossing the Sea, Refugee Camps, and Demonstrations. These reflect the traumatic circumstances defining forced migration today.

The plates use the language of traditional blue-and-white porcelain, while also referring to early Greek and Egyptian carvings and pottery. The plates' contemporary status is revealed upon closer inspection, with imagery sourced from the Internet and the artist's own experiences while filming the documentary feature *Human Flow* (2017).

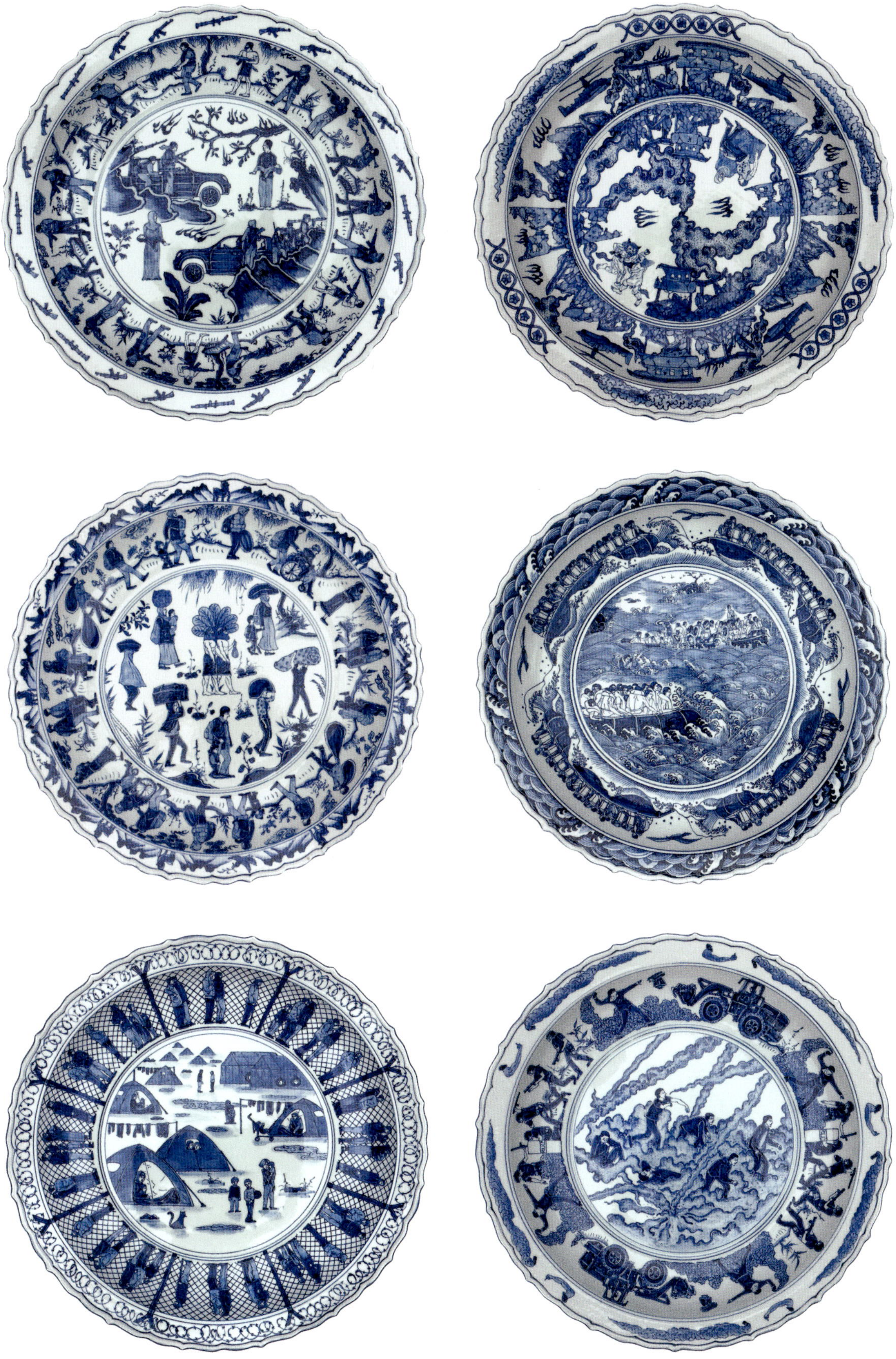

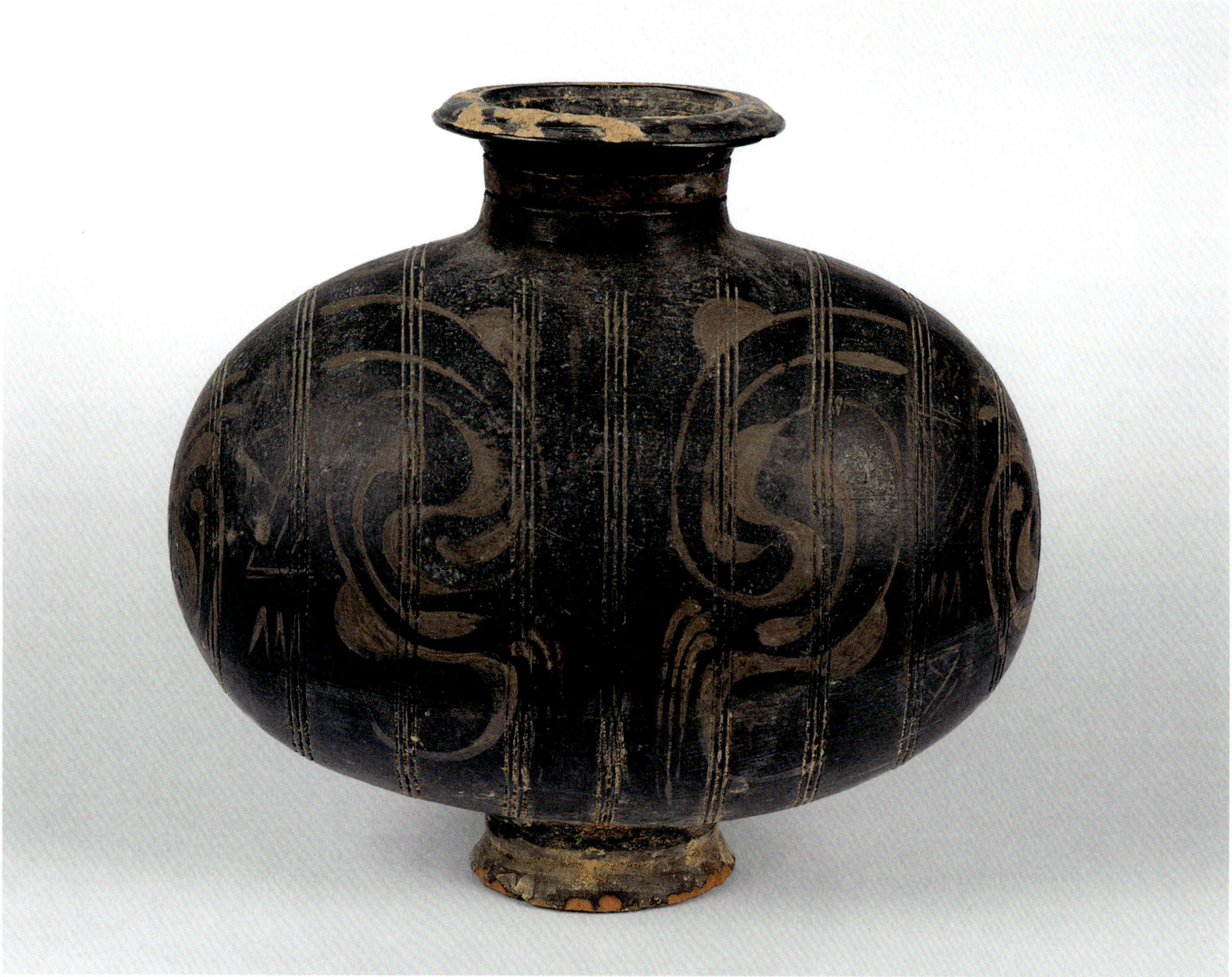

A Chinese painted pottery graduated 'cocoon' funerary jar
Earthenware, 30 × 32 cm, Han dynasty

Painted pottery jars of this form, known as 'cocoon' jars after the shape of silkworm cocoons, served as mortuary objects known as *mingqi*, or spirit vessels, in early China. They were placed in tombs together with many other funerary vessels, pottery figures and animals to serve the deceased in the afterlife. Jars of this type would have been used to store and serve liquid such as ale or water. The present example is noteworthy for its well-preserved decoration of interlacing and swirling clouds painted in coloured pigment. The decoration was placed on the jar to evoke the heavenly realm where the deceased was to cross once placed in the tomb. HE

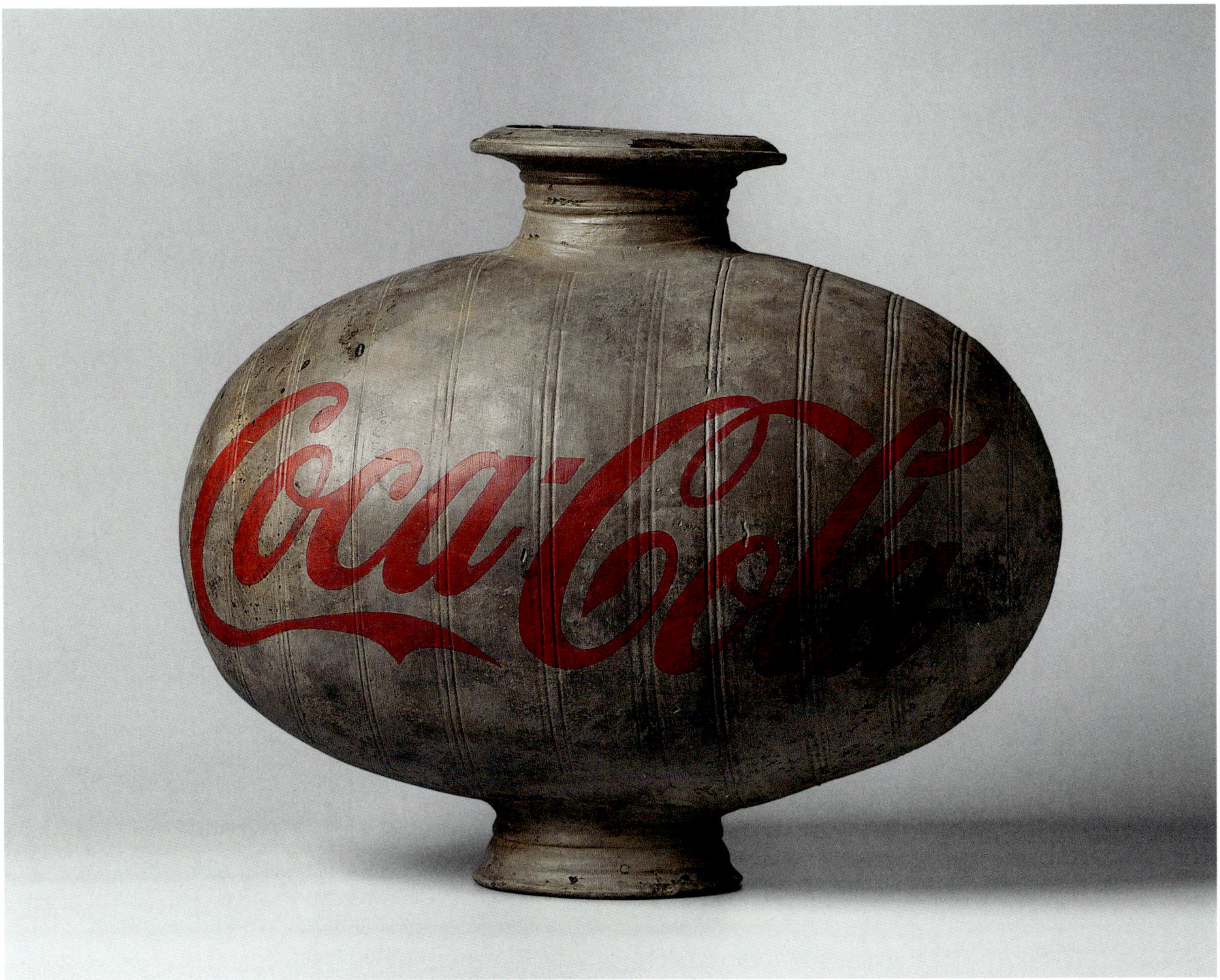

Han Dynasty Urn with Coca-Cola Logo, 2014
Han dynasty urn, paint, 27 × 28 cm

This urn is one of a series in which Ai has painted the Coca-Cola logo onto an ancient vessel. Burnishing a historical Chinese artefact with a globally recognisable brand, the artist considers the place of China within contemporary consumer culture.

The Chair of Non-attendance, 2013
Wood, 112 × 56 × 45 cm

The chair was made to commemorate a friend of Ai's who was detained by the Chinese state. It was presented in 2013 at the Stockholm Film Festival, where Ai had been invited to be a juror but was prevented from attending due to being barred from leaving China by state officials.

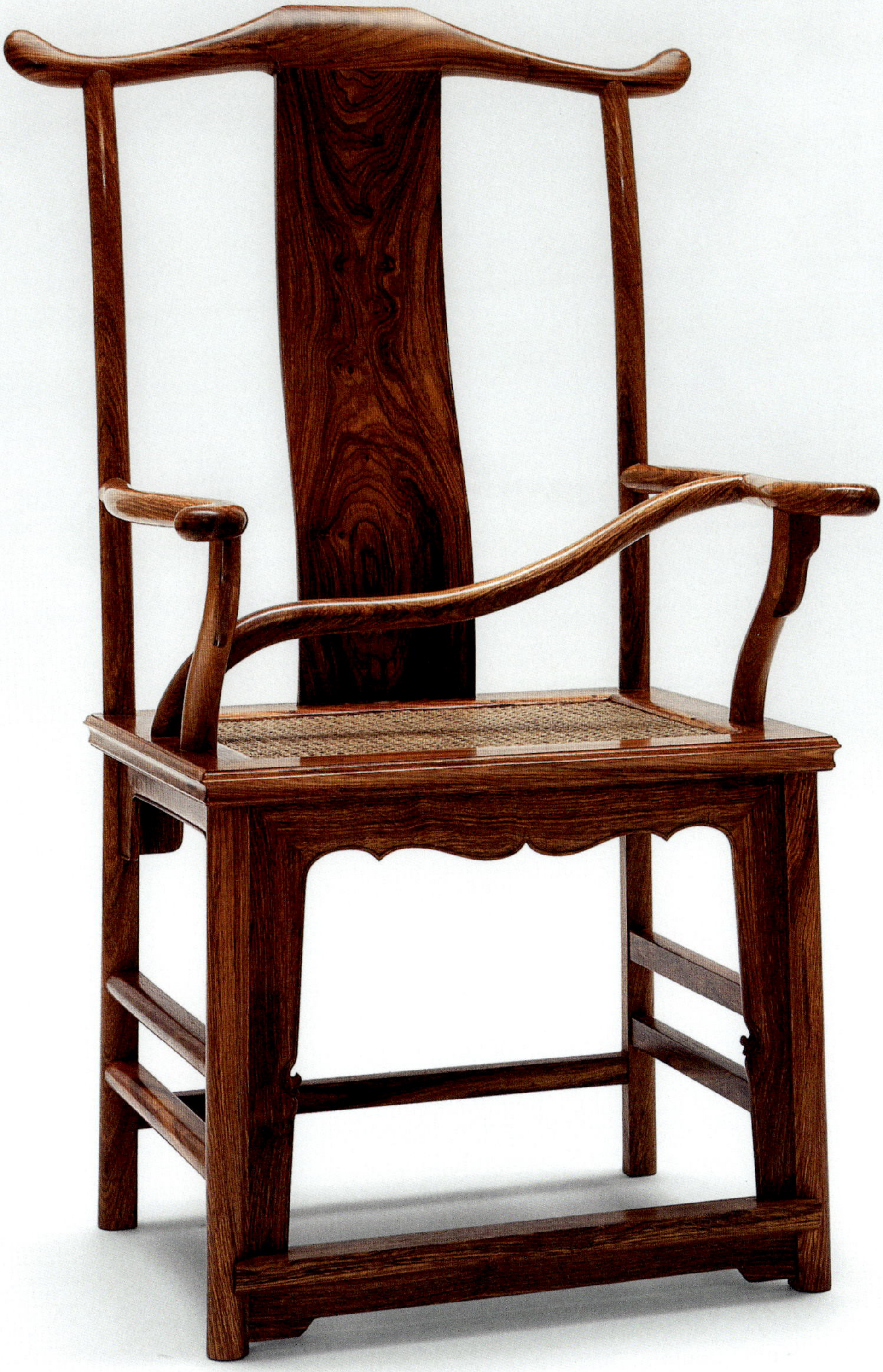

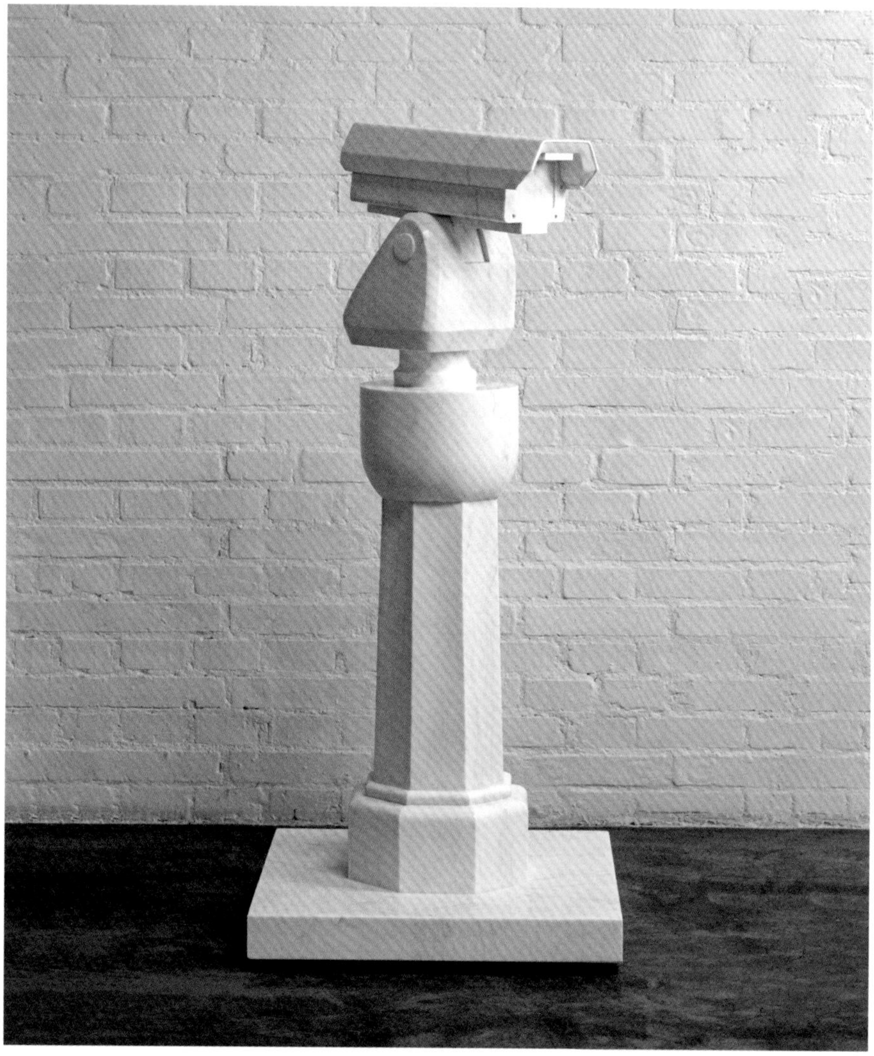

Surveillance Camera with Plinth, 2014
Marble, 120 × 52 × 52 cm

Since 2008, Ai's studio compound in Beijing has been surrounded by over two dozen surveillance cameras, put in place by the authorities. Following this intrusive act, Ai has frequently investigated the theme of surveillance in his work. *Surveillance Camera with Plinth* mimics a common camera with a base in the form of a pedestal oil-lamp in the style of the Northern Qi, usually placed in tombs. Combining ancient and modern design elements, Ai's work draws upon and questions the status of both.

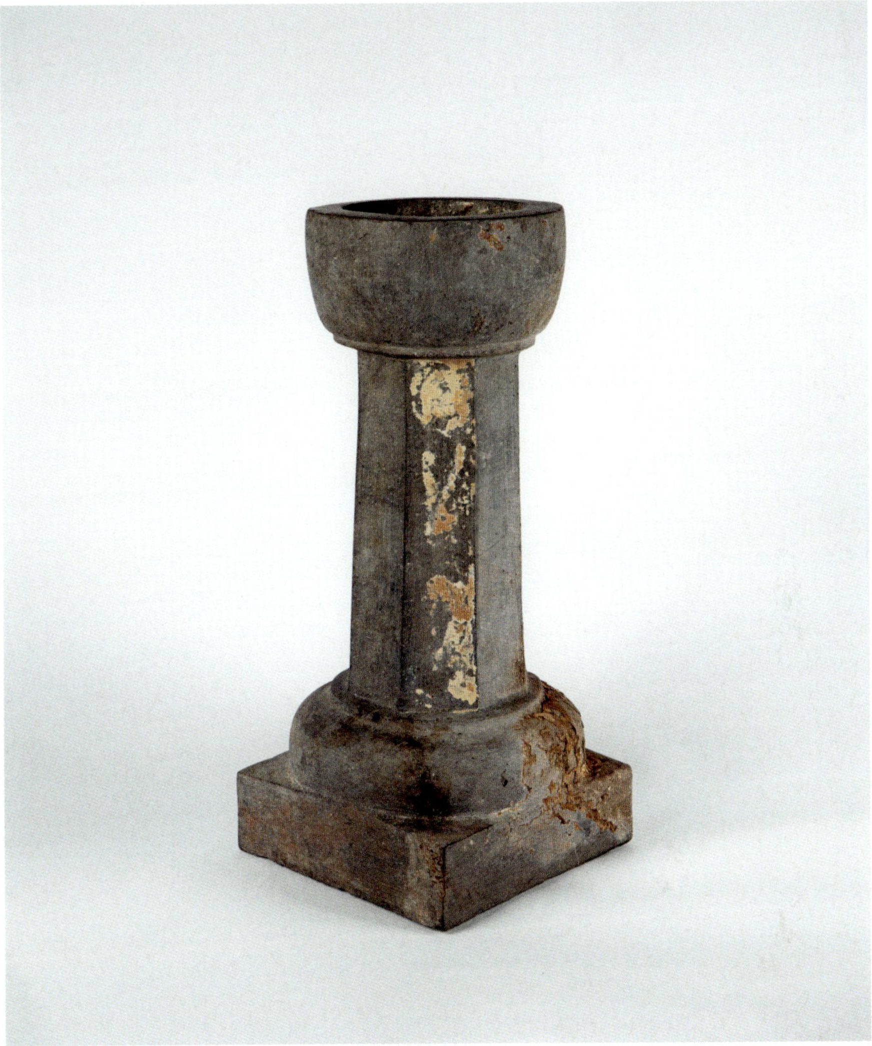

A Chinese black limestone pedestal oil lamp
Stone, height: 43.5 cm, perhaps Northern Wei dynasty

This tall oil lamp carved in limestone displays a clean architectural form made of a square base on which an octagonal column supports a large, round-shaped oil lamp. The combination of round and square forms refers to traditional Chinese cosmic symbolism evoking Heaven and Earth respectively. Related oil lamps were made in a variety of materials, such as bronze, ceramics, stone and wood, from as early as the Han dynasty. They would have been used for utilitarian purposes, lighted with the employment of vegetable oil or paraffin to fuel wicks that floated in the bowl. HE

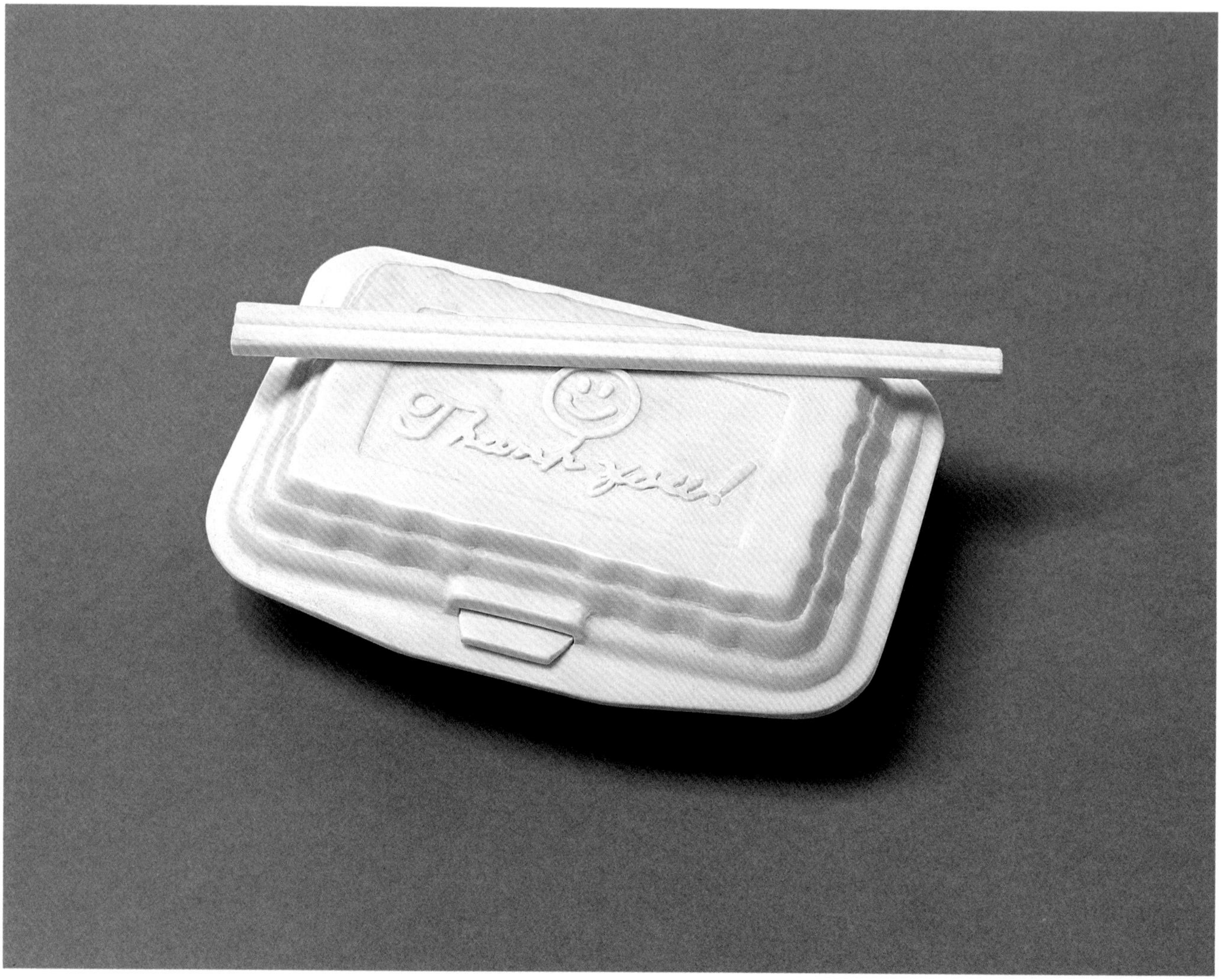

Marble Takeout Box, 2015
Marble, 7 × 19 × 14 cm

'The styrofoam takeout box is the most ubiquitous takeaway container in China, the most populous nation in the world. The work is a marker of this time of globalisation and the steep price China has paid, with regard to the health of its citizens through the exploitation of cheap labour, lack of protections for workers, and environmental destruction. Whereas China is the nation that has produced the highest quality porcelain in the past, indestructible styrofoam is widely used at the present time. Our time is characterised by single-use disposability and convenience. This will be written about in the history of globalisation, and the full effect will be passed on to the future.' — AI WEIWEI

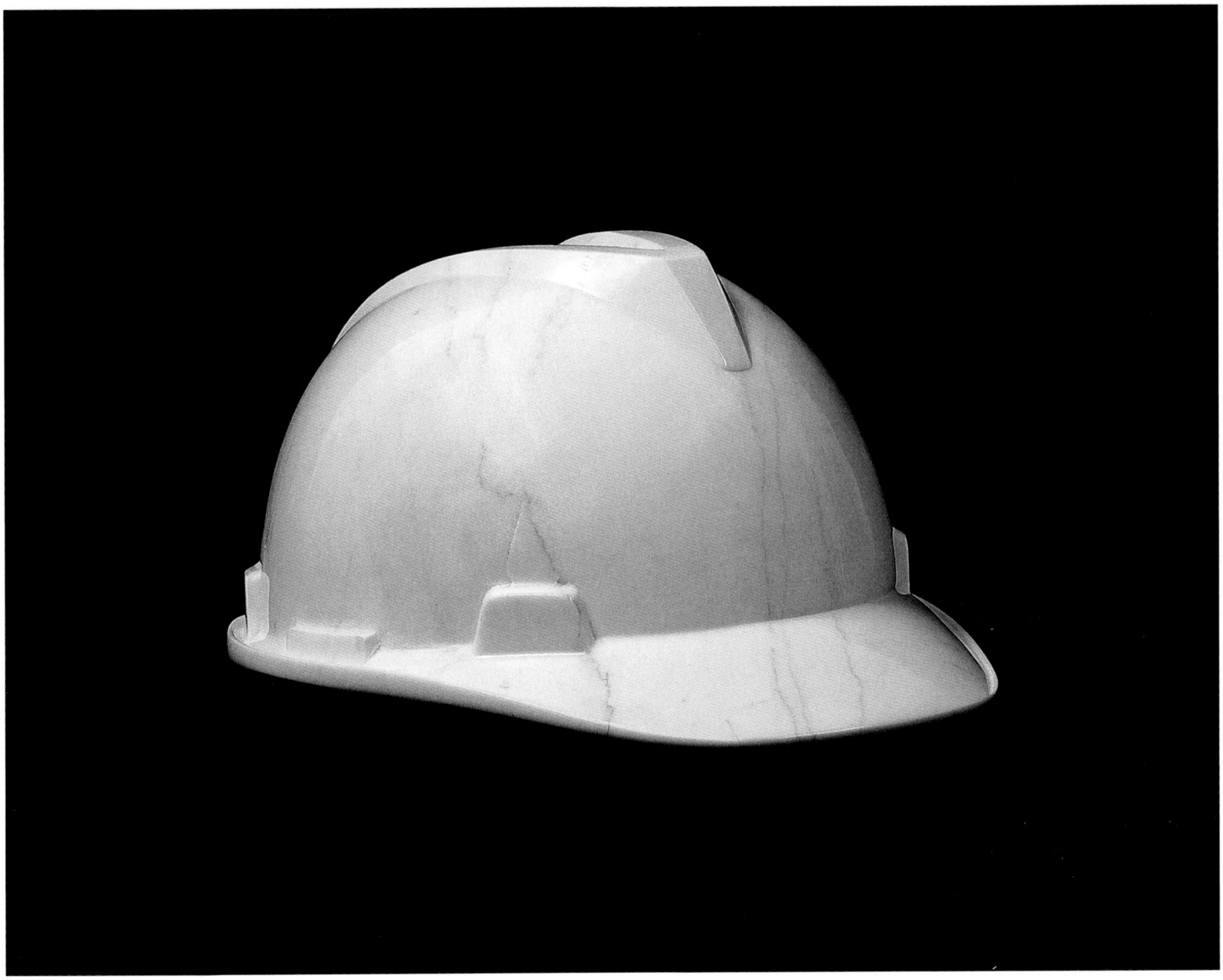

Marble Helmet, 2015
Marble, 15 × 28 × 18 cm

Ai has recreated a worker's hard-hat in marble. This type of protective helmet was used by those who tried to save the lives of those trapped under rubble in the days after the Sichuan earthquake of 2008, a disaster that Ai has addressed on many occasions in his work.

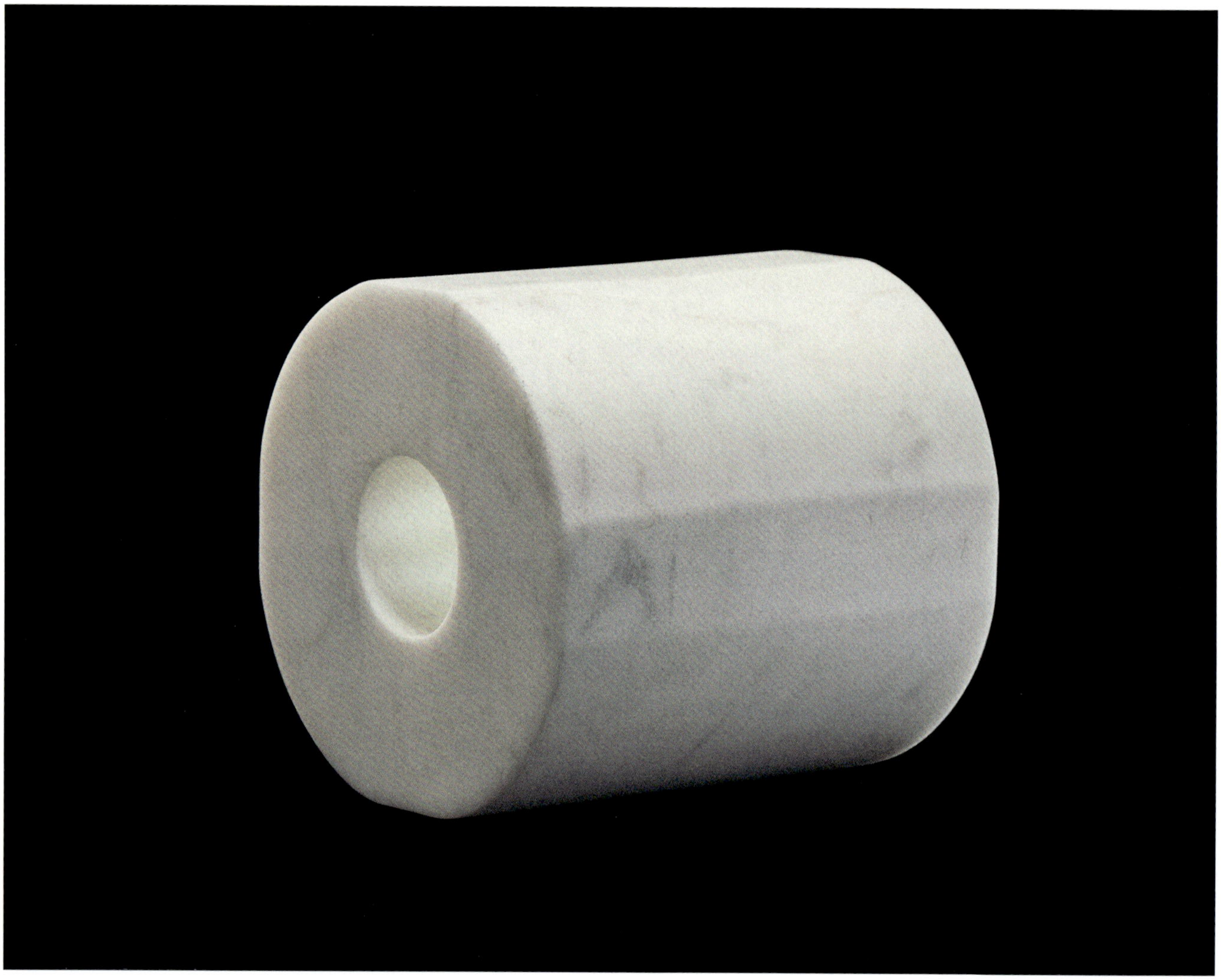

Marble Toilet Paper, 2020
Marble, 13.5 × 14 × 14 cm

'The whole world was in a panic in March 2020 due to the Covid-19 pandemic. Unnoticed and everyday objects suddenly became scarce in all the supermarkets. Toilet paper became symbolic of this time of panic and distrust. The work lays bare how fragile our so-called civilised progress actually is. The work is part of a series in marble, in the form of items which are essential to everyone's daily life yet ignored by the cultural landscape. These works, including *Mask* (2013), *Surveillance Camera with Plinth* (2014) and *Tyre* (2017), are testaments to our time.' — AI WEIWEI

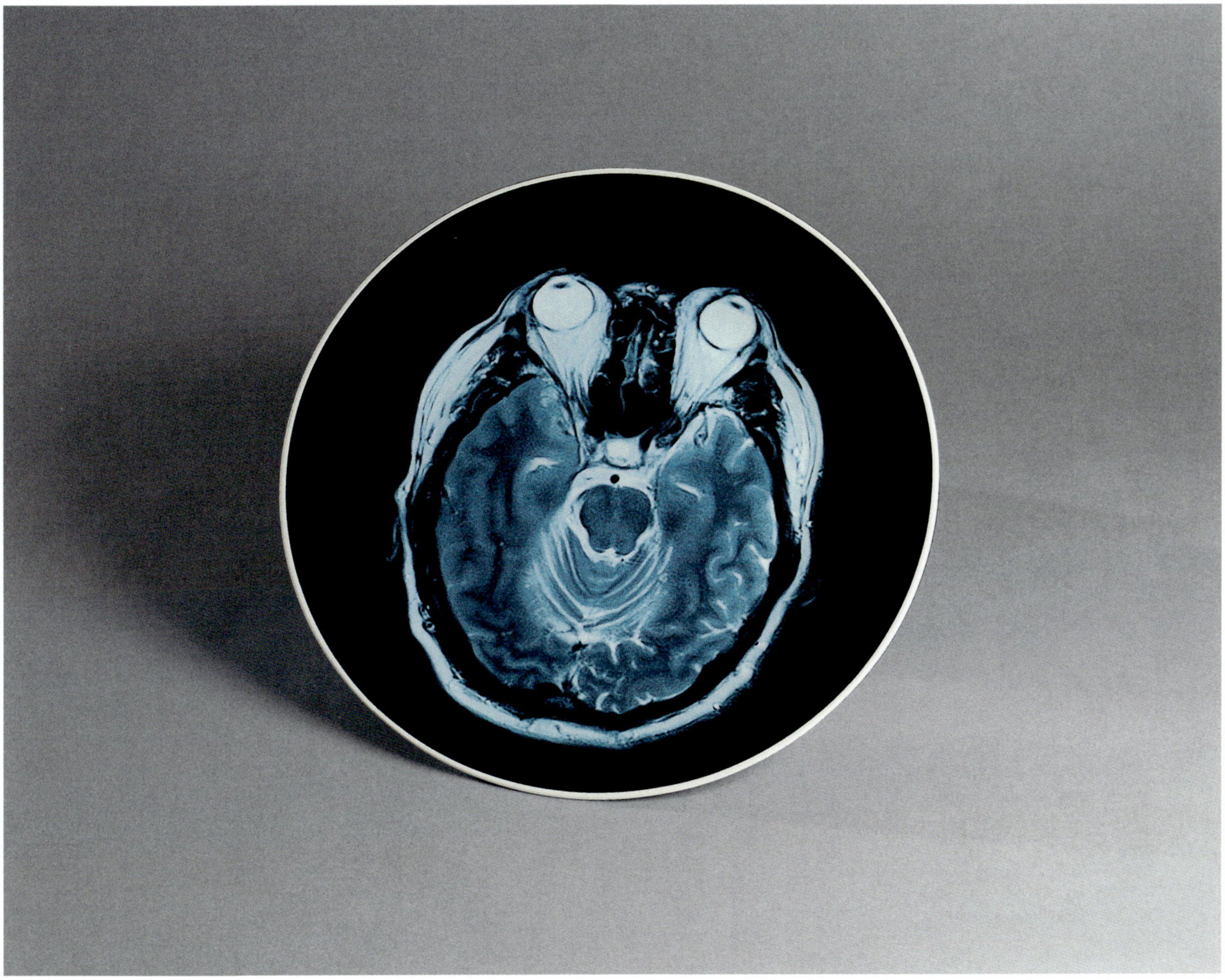

Brain Inflation, 2012
Porcelain, Ø 40 × 4.5 cm

The image on the plate is an MRI of Ai's brain showing the swelling that resulted from police violence. At the time of the attack, Ai had travelled to Chengdu to testify at the trial of Tan Zuoren, who had investigated the collapse of schools in the 2008 Sichuan earthquake and was charged with 'inciting subversion of state power'. The artist was prevented from leaving China until after the trial and was attacked by several policemen, which caused a cerebral haemorrhage and required him to undergo emergency brain surgery.

iPhone Cutout, 2015
Jade, 11.5 × 6 × 1 cm

Ai presents the silhouette of an early iPhone model carved in fine jade. A 'knock-off' of sorts made in a high-value material, the cutout holds a permanence that challenges smartphone culture, whereby consumers participate in a wasteful cycle of upgrading, replacing and discarding.

Cosmetics, 2013
Jade, set of 5, dimensions variable

Jade, a material prized in China for its value, durability and subtlety, is here used to present the throwaway plastic containers of cosmetics which, Ai notes, pile up in landfill and litter the oceans, and will never biodegrade.

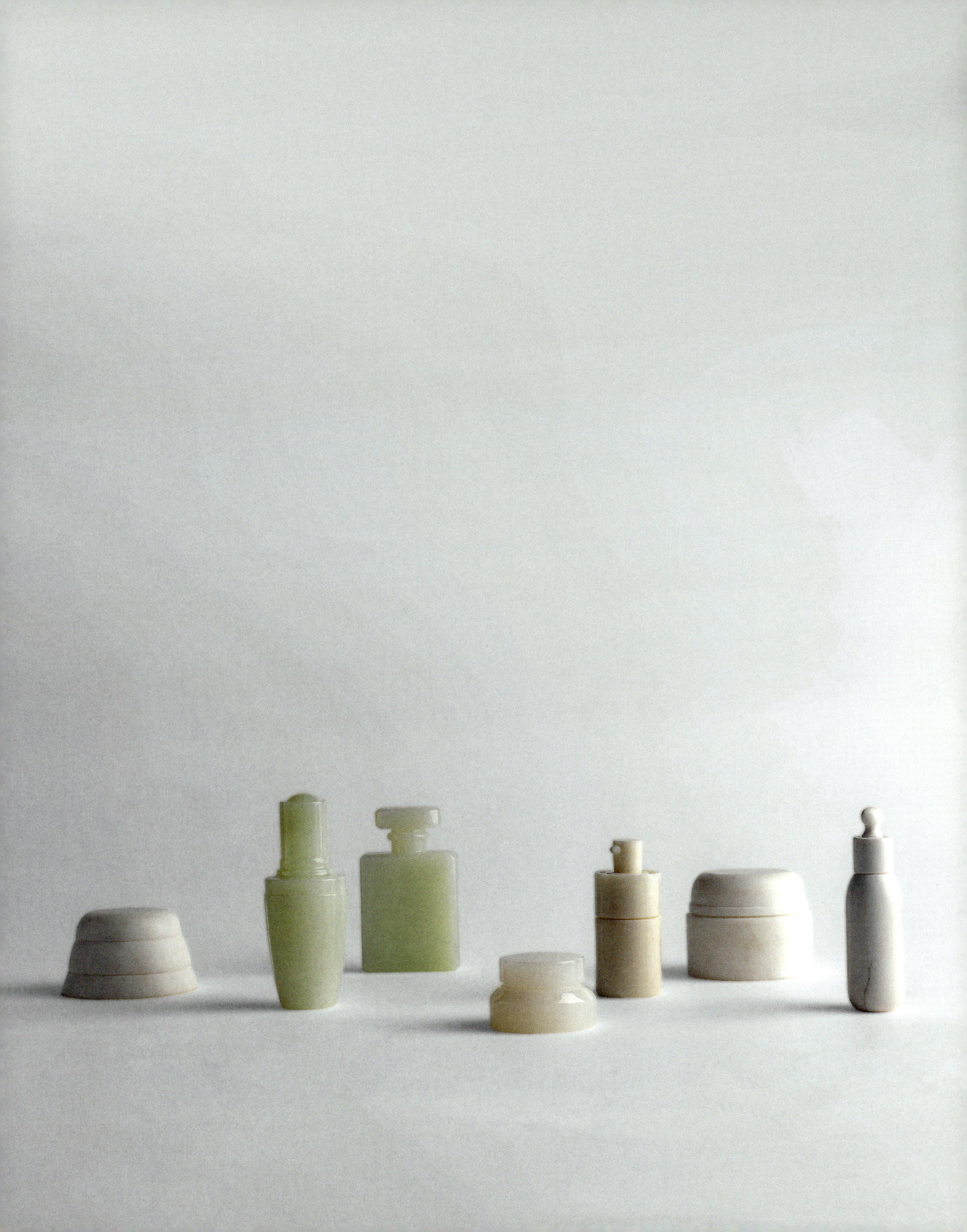

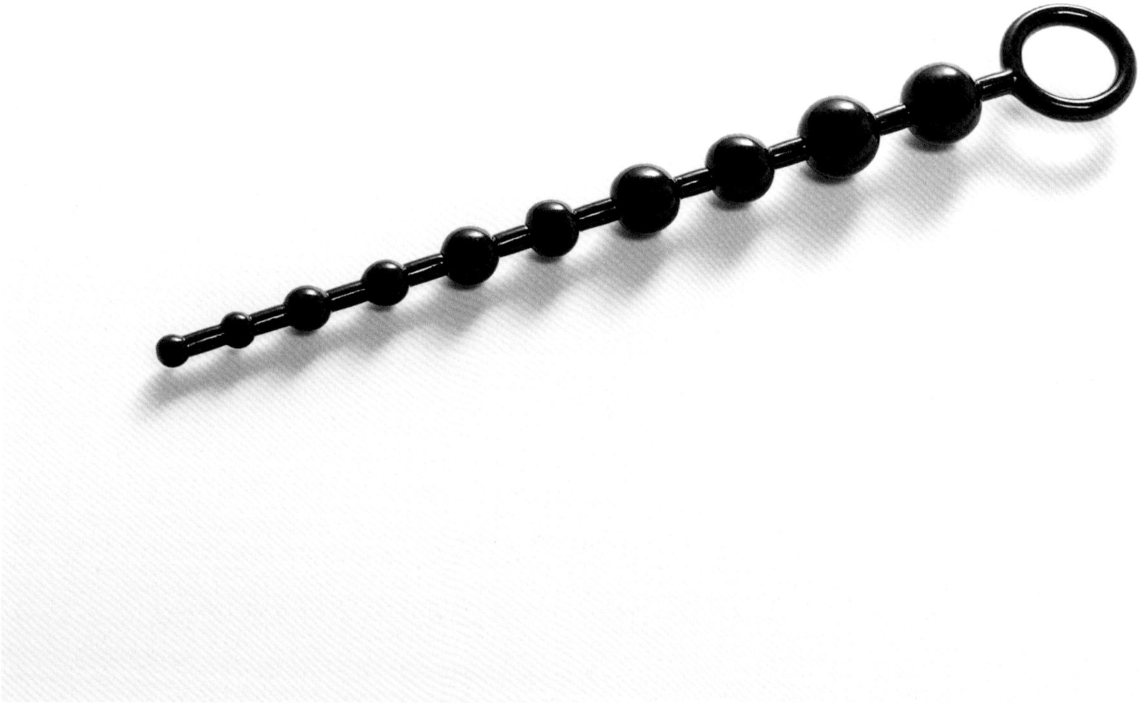

Sex Toy, 2014
Jade, 1 × 31 × 3 cm

Ai has used the valuable material of jade, associated with scholarly and cultural refinement, to create a replica of a sex toy. Marrying intimacy and eroticism, the artist challenges preconceptions of the work's medium as elevated and precious. At the same time, eroticism has often been a theme of artistic attention in Chinese history.

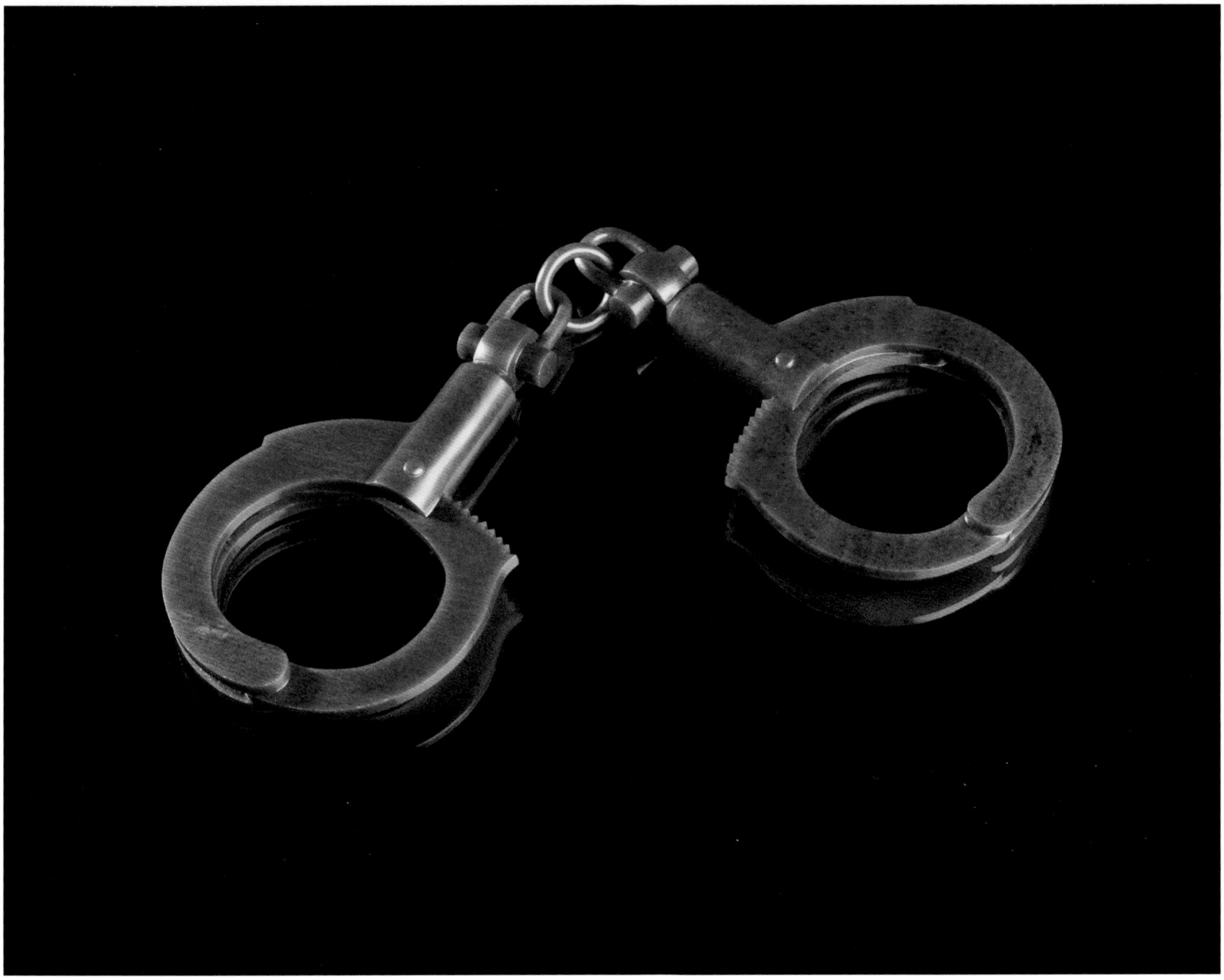

Handcuffs, 2011
Jade, 9 × 30 × 1.5 cm

Referring to Ai Weiwei's 2011 arrest and secret imprisonment in China for 81 days, these handcuffs are a symbol of oppression crafted from a single piece of fine jade.

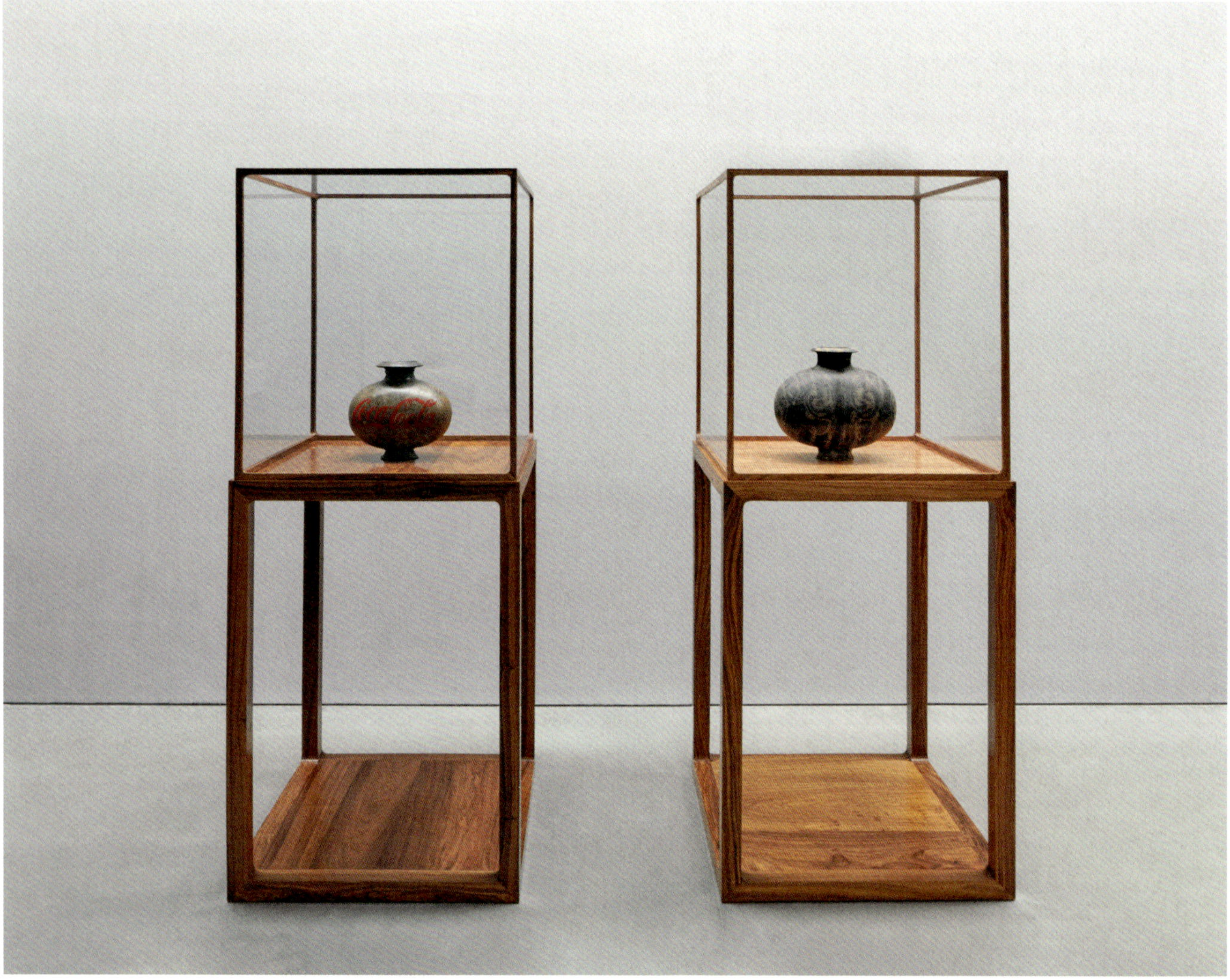

Display cases
Wood and glass, 175 × 70 × 70 cm each

Commissioned by Ai Weiwei, these museum-style cases were finely crafted to resemble those typically used to display jewellery or other highly valuable objects.

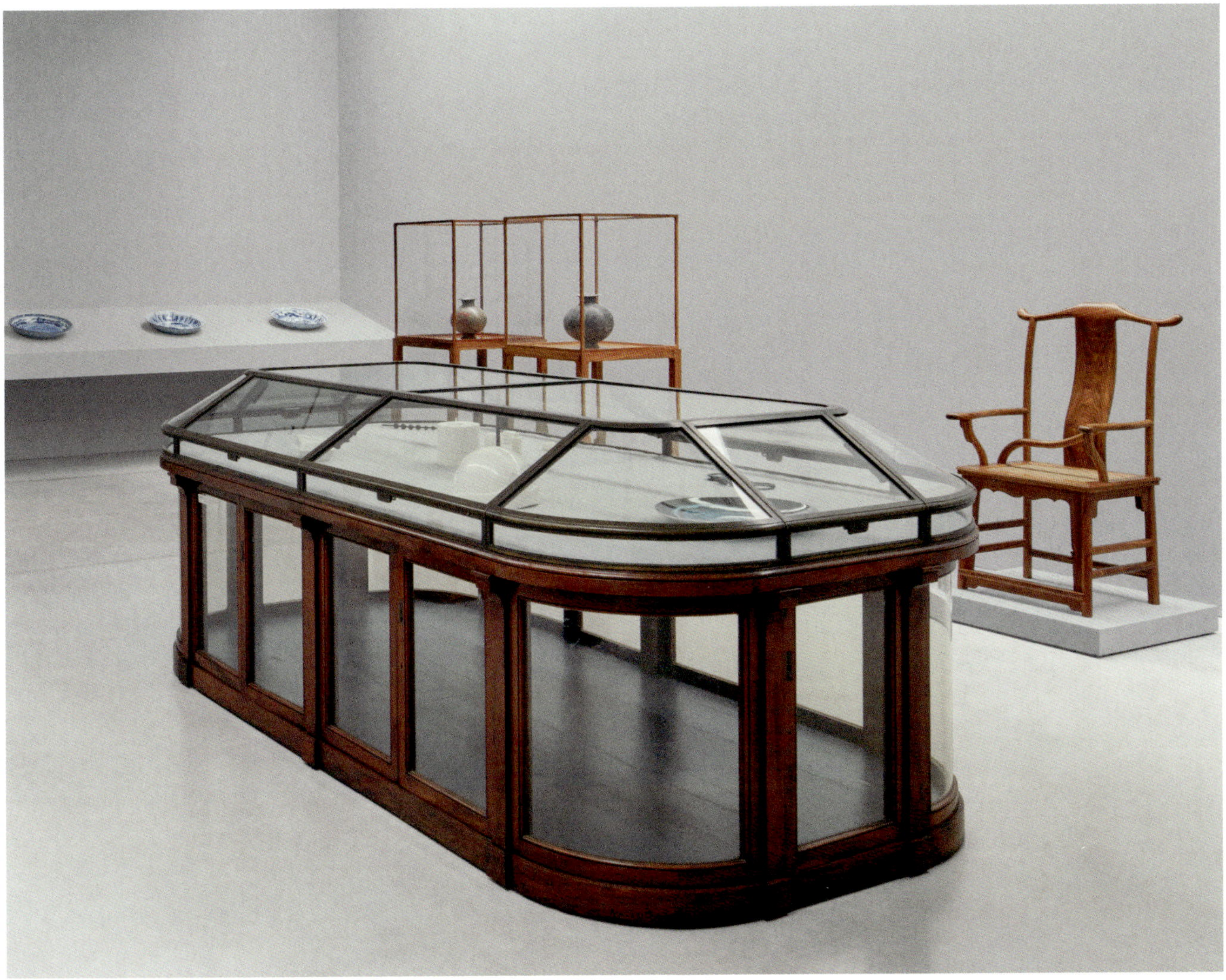

British Museum display case, early 20th century
Mahogany, brass, glass, fabric lining,
148 × 285 × 111 cm

This case was previously used by the British Museum and is now in the artist's collection. Dating from the early twentieth century, at the museum it was used for the display of Chinese earthenware.

Fairytale Chairs, 2007
Wood, set of 2, 105 × 56 × 44 cm each

These chairs were among the 1,001 wooden Qing dynasty chairs that the artist showed at the 12th *documenta* exhibition in Kassel, Germany (2007). For the occasion, Ai invited 1,000 Chinese nationals drawn from a wide cross-section of society to travel to Kassel, with the artist himself as the 1,001st participant. The chairs were distributed throughout the expansive exhibition sites, functioning as spaces to rest and reflect. The epic scale of the journey made by the participants, and the minutiae of their interactions with one another and the exhibition, unfolded in an environment shaped by the artist, who designed details ranging from participants' suitcases to their accommodation.

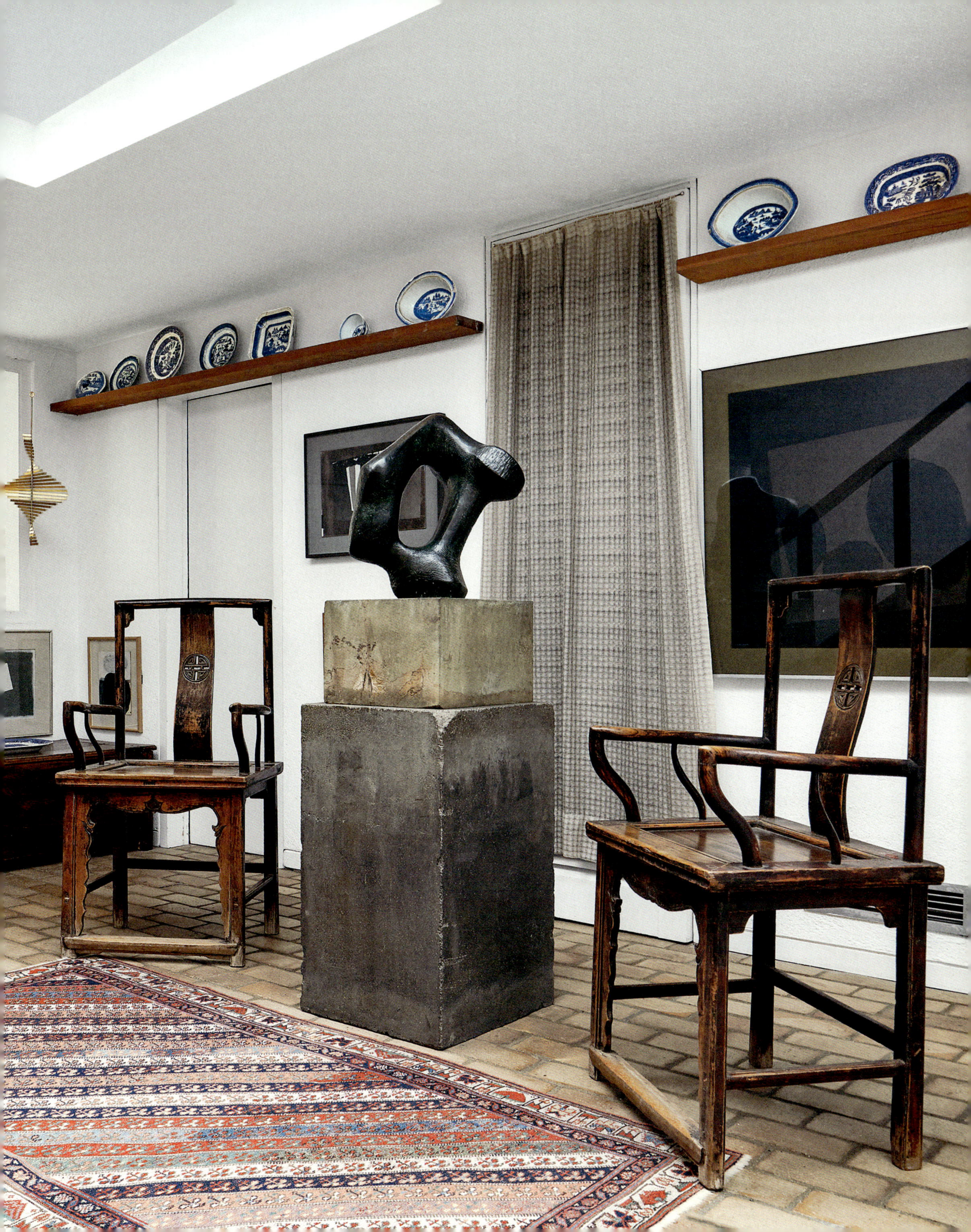

Black Cover Book / White Cover Book / Grey Cover Book, 1994–97
Softcover books, 25 × 21 × 2 cm each

Ai Weiwei is widely known as an artist and political activist, but his role as a pioneering publisher is often overlooked. After living in the United States for 12 years, Ai returned to China in 1993. He was met with questions from young artists, who, in a climate of government censorship and a near total lack of access to foreign art books, exhibition catalogues and art magazines, were eager for information about contemporary art. The books were ‘a means of communicating art conceptually and literally’, Ai Weiwei explained, and their dissemination underscored the presence of a large underground artists’ network in China.

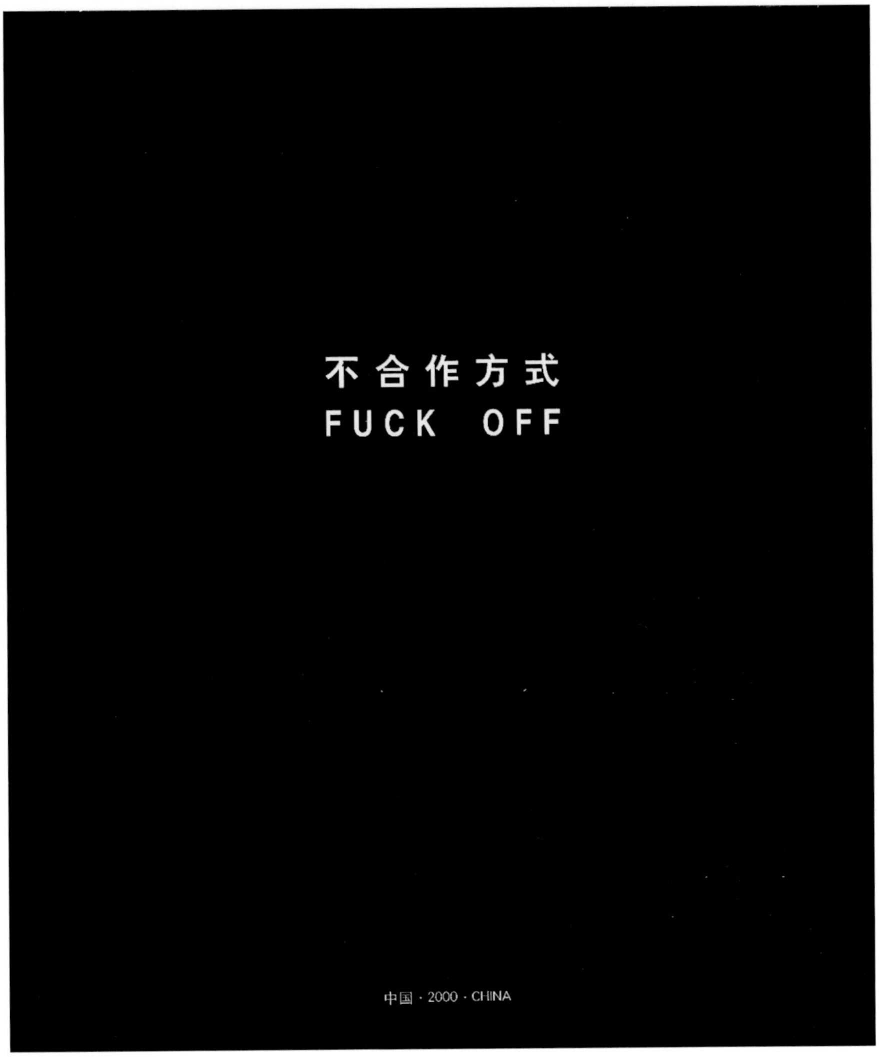

Fuck Off exhibition catalogue, 2000
Softcover book, 25 × 21 × 2 cm

In 2000, Ai Weiwei and co-curator Feng Boyi organised an independent exhibition titled *Fuck Off* in Shanghai. The exhibition ran alongside the Third Shanghai Biennale and featured the work of 46 contemporary artists from China. The curators' statement described the exhibition as emphasising 'the independent and critical stance that is basic to art's existence, and its status of independence, freedom and plurality in the situation of contradictions and conflicts.' The exhibition catalogue was self-published in an edition of 10,000.

Cats Wallpaper, 2015
Vinyl wallpaper, dimensions variable

Ai Weiwei's cats, whose names include Bai Bai, Din Din and Garfield, appear frequently in the artist's social media posts and he often mentions them in conversation. Many of the cats here are based on those who roamed the artist's former studio in Beijing. Two cats in black and white, drawn by Ai Weiwei and his son, Ai Lao, were added to the wallpaper recently and can be found in the centre of the image; they are called Maple and Birch.

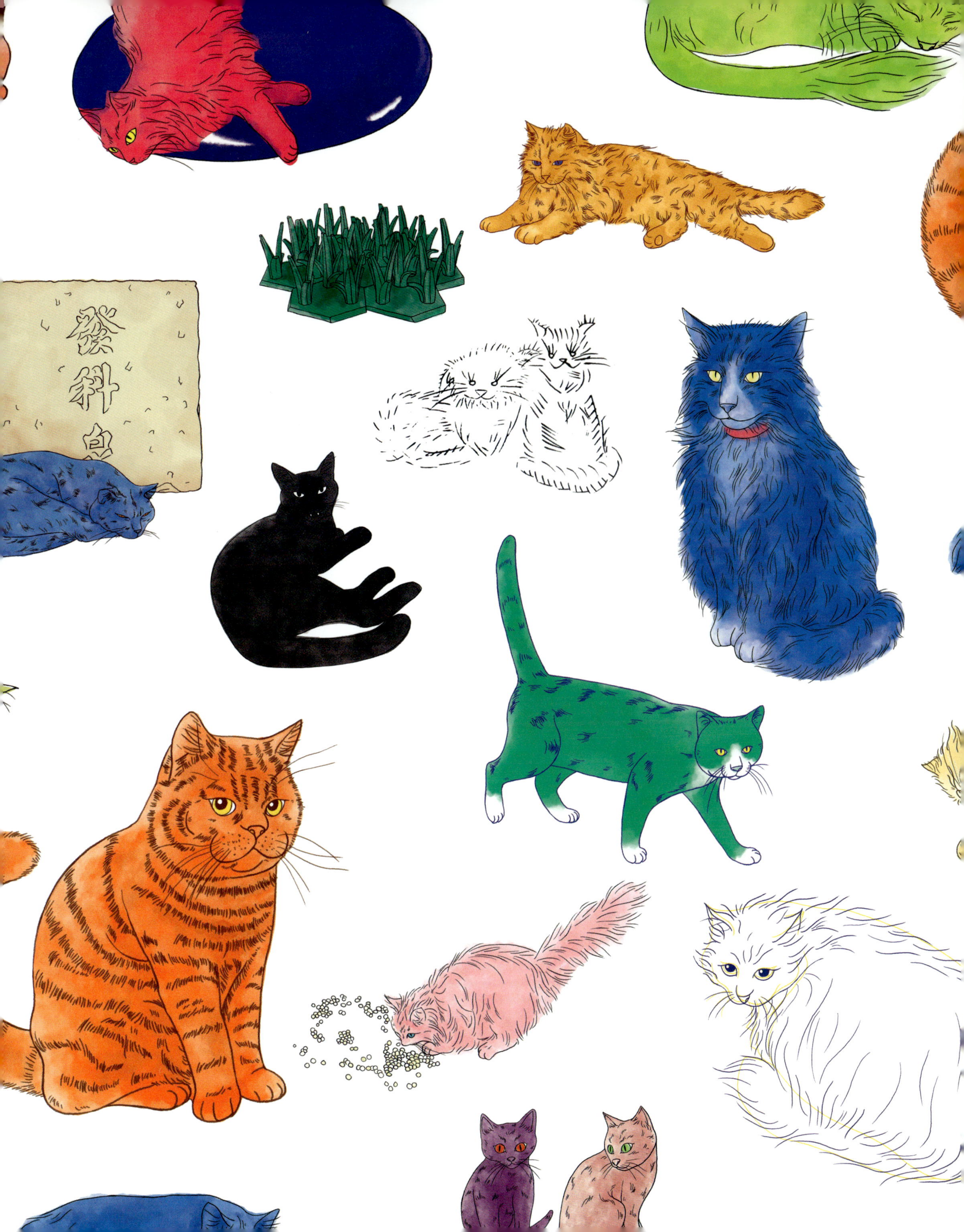

The Animal that Looks Like a Llama
But is Really an Alpaca, 2015
Vinyl wallpaper, dimensions variable

Motifs relating to issues of free speech and liberty can be made out in the wallpaper's design. Handcuffs, which may refer to Ai's imprisonment in China in 2011, are locked into concentric circles with surveillance cameras. The presence of the Twitter logo bird hints at censorship in China, as well as the global control that technology companies have to determine our access to reliable information and truth.

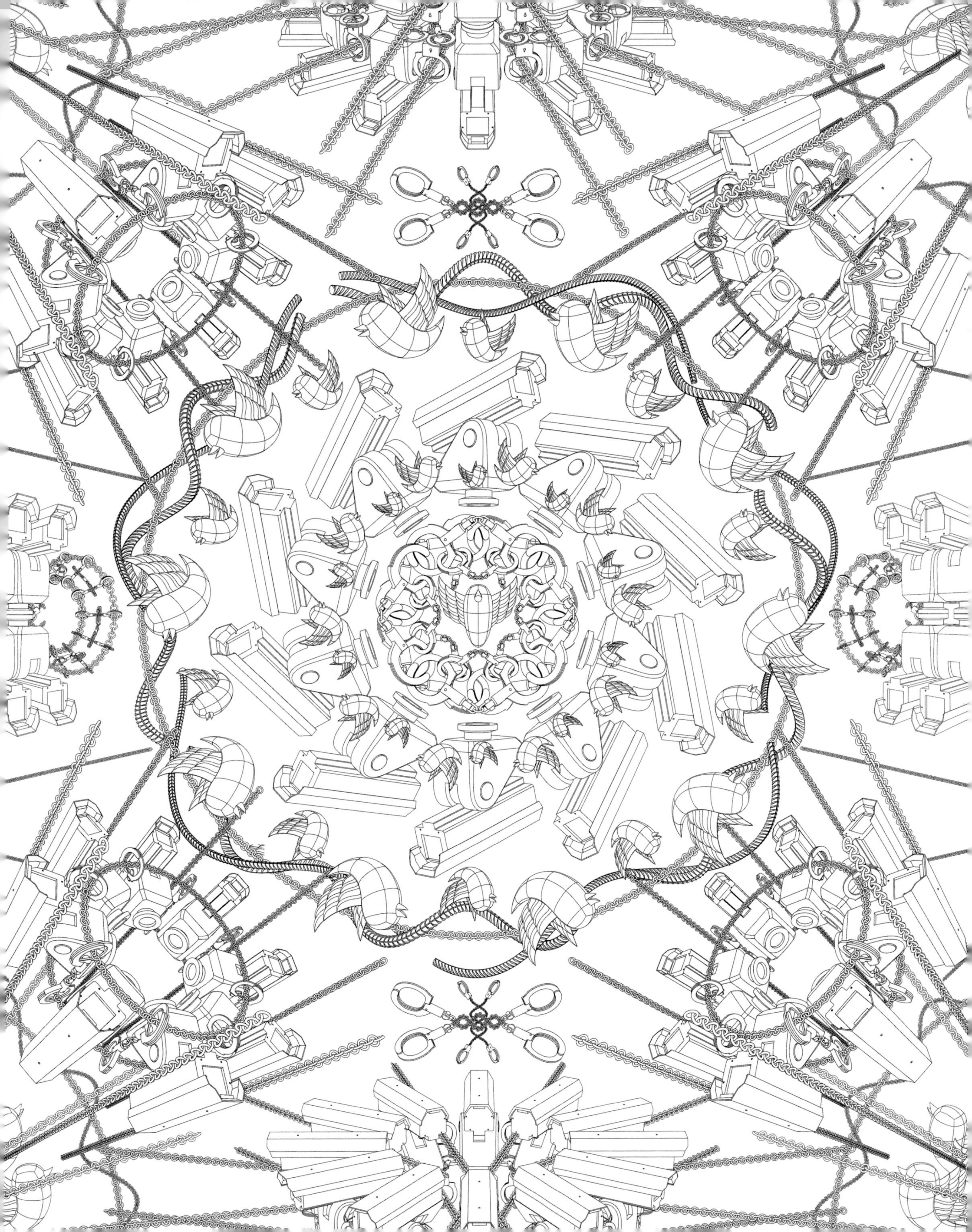

Finger, 2015
Vinyl wallpaper, dimensions variable

The outstretched arm and middle finger gesture is often found in Ai's work, including *Study of Perspective* (1995–2011) and *Arm with the Finger in Bronze* (2004). A profane sign inserted in public space, it suggests the artist's status as both dissident and playful provocateur.

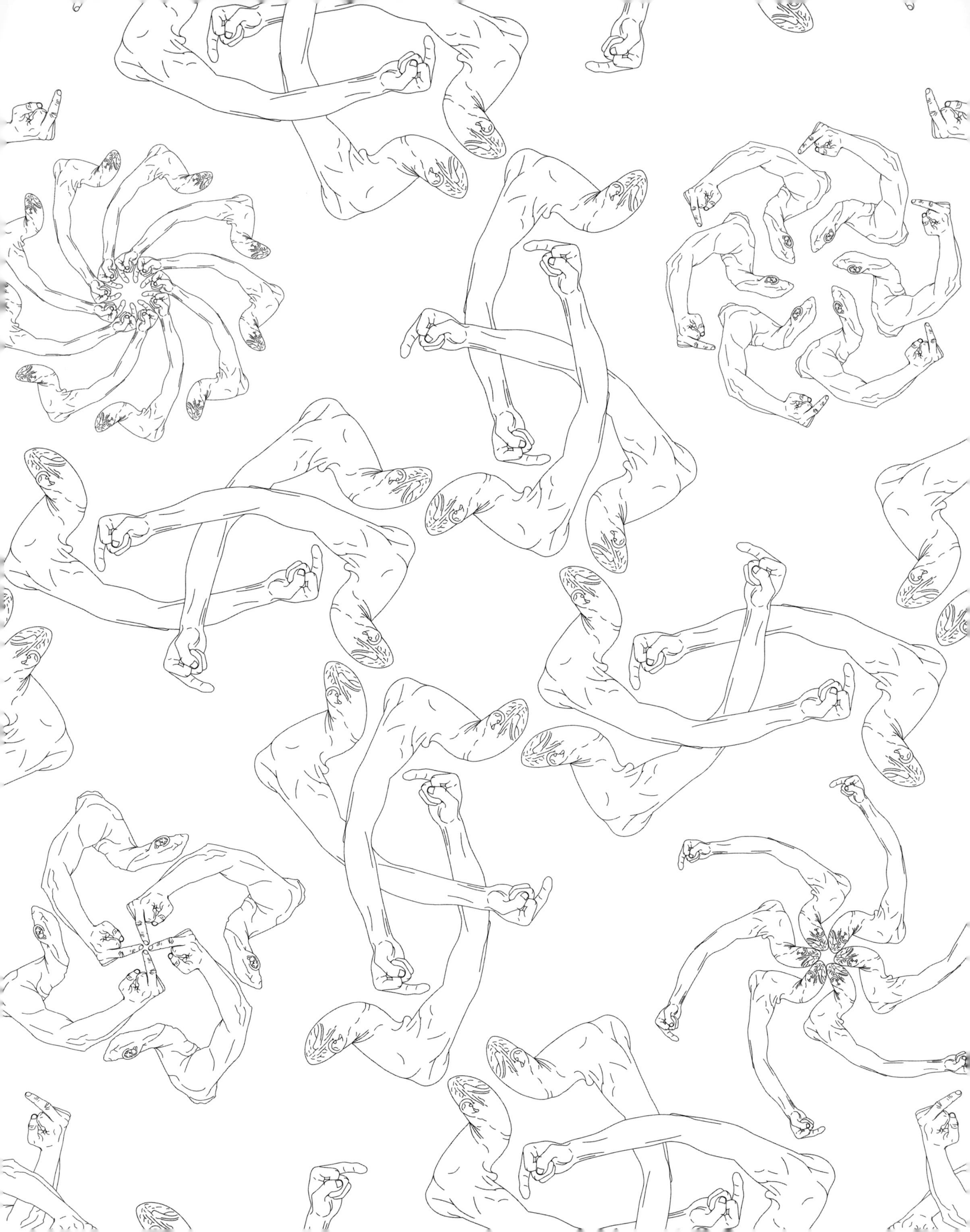

Coronation, 2020
Film, 113 minutes

Coronation is a documentary film about the lockdown in Wuhan, China, during the Covid-19 outbreak in the spring of 2020. Ai remotely directed and produced the film from Europe, and the filming was done by ordinary citizens living in Wuhan. On 1 December 2019, the first patient with Covid-19 symptoms was identified in Wuhan. Chinese officials repeatedly denied that human-to-human transmission was possible, concealed the number of diagnosed patients, and punished medical staff for disclosing information about the epidemic. On 23 January 2020, Wuhan was placed under a city-wide lockdown.

Through the lens of the pandemic, *Coronation* depicts the Chinese state crisis management and social control machine – through surveillance, ideological brainwashing and brute determination to control every aspect of society. The film shows the changes that took place in a city and in individual space under the impact of the virus; it illustrates the value of individual life in the political environment, reflecting on the difficulties we face as individuals and countries in the context of globalisation. Ultimately, the result is a society lacking trust, transparency and respect for humanity. Despite the impressive scale and speed of the Wuhan lockdown, we face a more existential question: can civilisation survive without humanity? Can nations rely on one another without transparency or trust?

Human Flow, 2017
Film, 145 minutes, courtesy Altitude.film

Over 65 million people around the world have been forced from their homes to escape famine, climate change and war in the greatest human displacement since the Second World War. *Human Flow*, an epic film journey led by Ai Weiwei, gives a powerful visual expression to this massive human migration. The documentary elucidates both the staggering scale of the refugee crisis and its profoundly personal human impact.

Captured over the course of an eventful year in 23 countries, the film follows a chain of urgent human stories that stretches across the globe in countries including Afghanistan, Bangladesh, France, Greece, Germany, Iraq, Israel, Italy, Kenya, Mexico and Turkey. *Human Flow* is a witness to its subjects and their desperate search for safety, shelter and justice: from refugee camps to perilous ocean crossings to barbed-wire borders; from dislocation and disillusionment to courage, endurance and adaptation; from the haunting lure of lives left behind to the unknown potential of the future. *Human Flow* represents a crucial time when tolerance, compassion and trust are needed more than ever. This visceral work of cinema is a testament to the unassailable human spirit and poses one of the questions that will define this century: will our global society emerge from fear, isolation and self-interest and choose a path of openness, freedom and respect for humanity?

Cockroach, 2020
Film, 93 minutes

This documentary film bears witness to the protests in Hong Kong in 2019. In February 2019, the Hong Kong government proposed a bill to allow extradition of criminal suspects from Hong Kong to face trial in mainland China. The controversial bill sparked immediate outrage over widespread fear of arbitrary detention and politically motivated trials that would decimate Hong Kong's autonomy under 'one country, two systems'. Anti-bill protests escalated into pro-democracy demonstrations.

Cockroach, filmed during the height of the protests, captures the extraordinary intensity of an unprecedented era in Hong Kong's history. Spanning the evolution of the protest movement, it captures street demonstrations, police suppression and violence, and key events such as the multi-day siege of Hong Kong Polytechnic University. Interviews with Hong Kongers feature activists, protestors, politicians, ordinary citizens and police officers. Prominent legislators, lawyers and activists articulate the perils of intensifying assaults on freedoms and rule of law.

Cockroach is a dramatic visual record of the final moments of an independent, democratic Hong Kong. On 30 June 2020, China imposed the National Security Law in Hong Kong, effectively ending Hong Kong's judicial and political independence and placing the city firmly under Beijing's control.

GLOSSARY

BODHISATTVA

An enlightened being who seeks awakening and is on the path of becoming a Buddha.

BODHISATTVA AVALOKITESHVARA

One of the most important deities in Buddhism. Vowing to liberate all beings in the universe from pain and suffering, he remains on earth deferring his own enlightenment.

BUDDHISM

Buddhism is a religion founded more than 2,500 years ago in India by Siddhartha Gautama, known as the Buddha. Followers of Buddhism focus on achieving enlightenment, a state of inner peace and wisdom.

DAOISM

Daoism is one of the most important religious and philosophical systems in China. It emphasises living in harmony with nature, which is also known as the *Dao*, or Way.

ENLIGHTENMENT

In Buddhism, enlightenment represents a state of achievement of perfect knowledge or wisdom, combined with infinite compassion.

HAN DYNASTY

China's second Imperial dynasty, which ruled from 206 BCE to 220 CE. It promoted the philosophy of Confucianism, opened up foreign trade along the Silk Road and permanently changed China's political, social, economic and cultural landscape over 400 years.

HISTORICAL BUDDHA

Also known as Shakyamuni Buddha or Siddhartha Gautama, the Buddha was a religious leader and teacher in India and attained enlightenment under the Bodhi Fig Tree.

LAOZI

An ancient Chinese philosopher and founder of Daoism, and the reputed author of the sixth-century primary text of Daoism, the *Daode jing* (Classic of the Way and Virtue).

MAITREYA BUDDHA

The future Buddha of this world, who as a bodhisattva resides in Heaven and will descend to preach the *dharma* (law) when the teachings of Siddhartha Gautama, the historical Buddha, have completely decayed.

NORTHERN WEI DYNASTY

The Northern Wei dynasty (386–534 CE) was ruled by the Tuoba people and was one of China's most significant northern dynasties before the reunification under the Sui dynasty.

NORTHERN QI DYNASTY

One of the northern dynasties, the Northern Qi (550–577 CE) was founded by Emperor Wenxuan and covered the lower region of the Yellow River, modern day Shanxi and the northern parts of Jiangsu and Anhui provinces.

QING DYNASTY

China's last dynasty in its Imperial history, the Qing dynasty was ruled by the Manchus from northeast China from 1644 to 1911.

SUI DYNASTY

The Sui dynasty (581–618 CE) is significant in Chinese history for reuniting northern and southern China after nearly four centuries of political fragmentation. It set up important institutions that were adopted by its successor, the Tang dynasty (618–906 CE).

BY DR HAJNI ELIAS

REAL VS. FAKE

JAMES J. LALLY

What is the difference between a genuine work of art and a fake or a copy? The response to this deceptively simple question has evolved very differently in China than in the West, especially in the high art of painting.

Since the Renaissance in Europe, artists, collectors and art historians have emphasised the original work as the true essence of the artist's genius and regarded all copies as inferior and undesirable. In the Western tradition the accurate determination of age and authorship is absolutely critical to understanding and appreciating the quality of any work of art. Copies and replicas of works of art are regarded as lacking the special creativity of the original and therefore fundamentally inferior. Unique works of art by the best artists of any age are cherished as precious, inviolable repositories of truth and beauty. Copies and fakes are at best secondary and generally irrelevant. From this point of view, the best fakes are the most offensive because they have the highest potential to obscure the truth and mislead the viewer.

In China, the attitude towards fakes and copies is more complex and nuanced. Throughout the history of painting in China, copying and close imitation was the approved method of developing a deep understanding of the styles and techniques of the master painters of the past. Aspiring artists diligently produced careful copies of the classic paintings of famous artists and many accomplished Chinese artists continued to paint copies and re-interpretations of classic masterworks throughout their careers.

For painters in the Chinese classical tradition, copying is not just a method of learning, it is an intrinsically valid and valuable creative activity, acknowledging the authority of the past and entering into a conversation with the masters. The purpose of copying a classic painting or calligraphy in China is not the production of an exact replica; rather it is an exercise in homage done in the spirit of participating in an ongoing tradition. The best analogy to this concept is the performance of an accomplished musician playing a classic composition – the notes are the same but each performance is a different interpretation of the composition.

Collecting ancient art has a long history in China. In the Song dynasty (960–1279) there was already a well-developed appreciation of ancient bronze ritual vessels, jades and other artefacts unearthed from Neolithic and Bronze Age sites. The Song dynasty emperors formed large collections of antiquities. The scholar-elite of the Imperial bureaucracy quickly followed the emperor's lead, and the market expanded. The supply of genuine antiquities was limited, and soon fakes and copies of ancient objects were made. Some copies were presented as neoclassical revivals in the style of ancient art, but many copies were sold as real antiquities. Collecting continued through succeeding dynasties, and by the Ming dynasty (1368–1644) the production of copies and fakes was rife. The makers were not acting in the same spirit as Chinese painters, seeking to continue an artistic tradition and enter into a conversation with the past; rather they were anonymous craftspeople producing commercial goods for sale.

Because of the long tradition of including copies and fakes in the artistic practice of Chinese painting and calligraphy, some observers contend that the same attitude naturally extends into the realm of Chinese antiquities, such as copies of Chinese ritual bronzes, archaic jades and sculpture, but I do not subscribe to that point of view. In my experience the attitude towards fake antiquities in China is very similar to the Western attitude: a 'real' ancient or antique work of art is the product of a specific time and place and serves a specific purpose in a specific historical context. A 'fake' work is an imitation of the antique, made to deceive the viewer.

In some museums in China, exact reproductions of ancient artworks, or *fuzhipin*, are exhibited, and some Chinese museum personnel have told me they believe those modern reproductions are identical with the original excavated antiquities, not 'fakes'. But the great majority of Chinese curators, scholars and collectors I have met are keenly aware of the distinction between an original artwork and a later copy, agreeing that authenticity and age are key to value.

Today the market for Chinese antiquities of all kinds is larger than ever before. Copies of ancient bronzes, archaic jade carvings, ceramics and sculptures are being produced in significant quantities. These copies and fakes are a falsification of the historical record, potentially misleading scholars and collectors seeking a deeper understanding and appreciation of the arts of the past.

The best way – some might even say the only way – to develop a reliable understanding and appreciation of the arts of ancient China is by careful study of genuine artworks, constantly comparing original examples from reliable sources to learn how to recognise the aesthetics, styles, materials, techniques and function of specific antiquities in their original context. A scientific analysis or test carefully applied can sometimes be helpful in determining the age or the authenticity of an object, but in my experience hands-on examination and old-fashioned connoisseurship is always rewarding and often essential.

To understand and appreciate ancient art, the genuine ancient art objects in museums and old collections are the best source of reliable information. It is often said someone adept at spotting fakes and copies 'has a good eye', but it is very important to use all your senses, not just your eyes, when examining an object, and it is essential to study the actual object. Photographs of art objects can be of some use, but they can also be misleading. The surface texture, the weight, the balance, the natural wear on the surface and other revealing information will not be well understood until you have the object in your hands. Close inspection of the best genuine examples you can find will provide a guide to how the object was made, what materials and techniques were employed, what shapes and proportions were popular at the time and other data to use for comparison with examples of the same type. The best method of developing connoisseurship is a constant process of comparing salient characteristics of the object in hand with similar examples, placing the objects side-by-side whenever possible, but often relying on your memory bank. In addition to the aesthetic criteria relating to how the object was designed to look when it was made, other practical information about how the object was originally used and what kind of natural wear or surface corrosion may be expected can be enlightening. Examination, study and analysis of actual objects is the best way to learn and appreciate the difference between the finest works of art and all the rest. Learning to recognise the copies and fakes is naturally a small part of that never-ending process.

Whether you love fakes or hate them, there will always be fakes and copies in the art world.

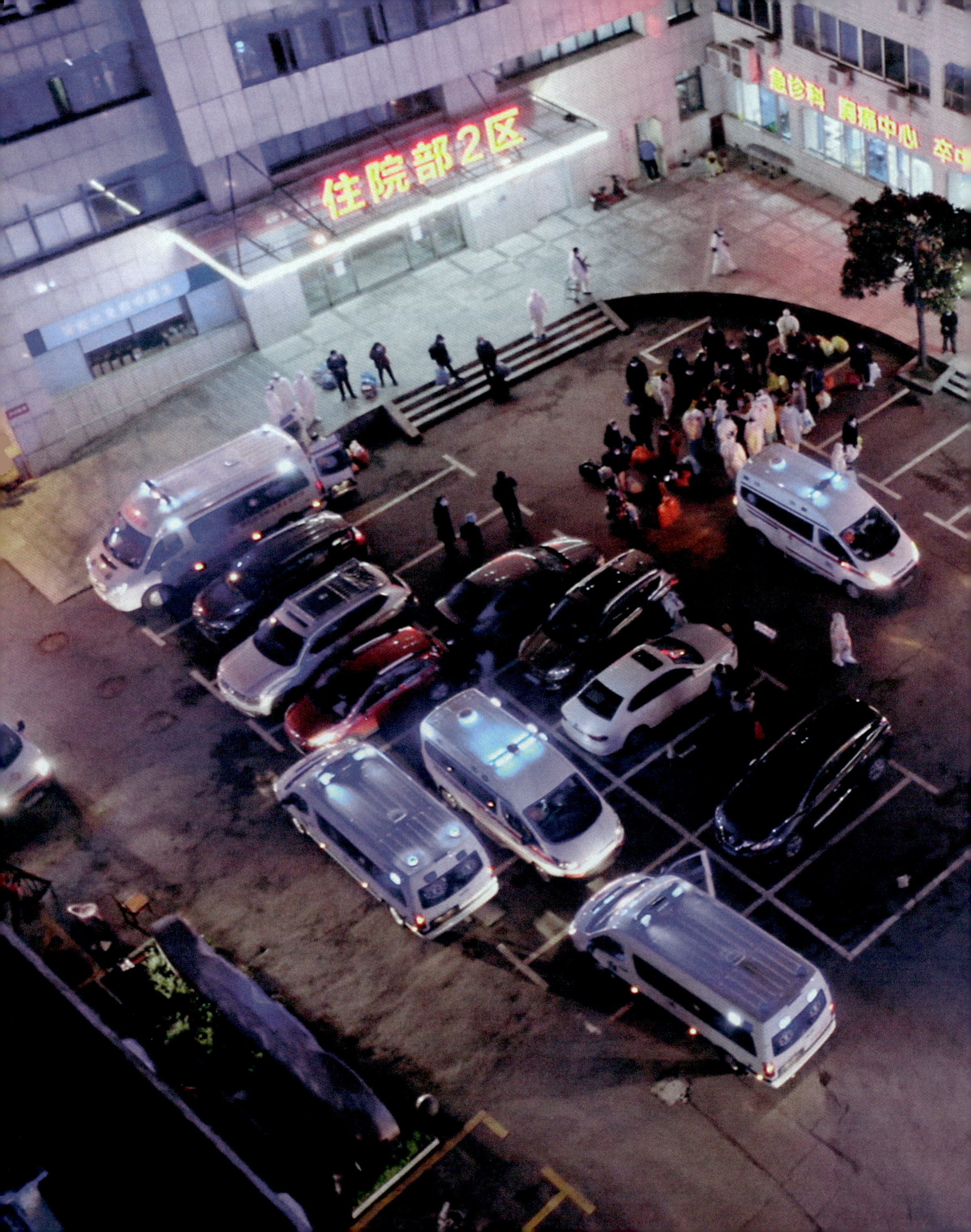
住院部2区
急诊科

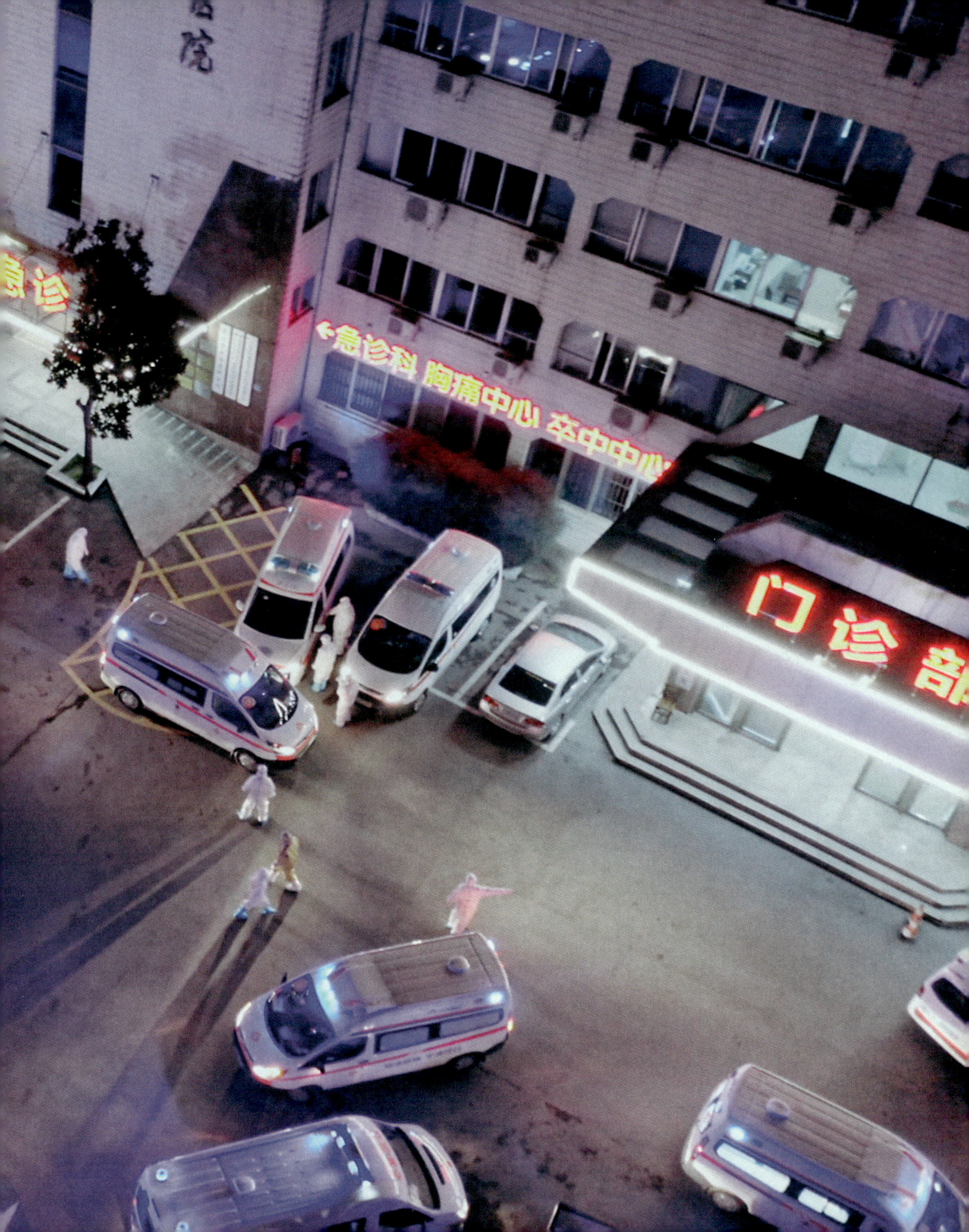
急诊科 胸痛中心 卒中中心
门诊部

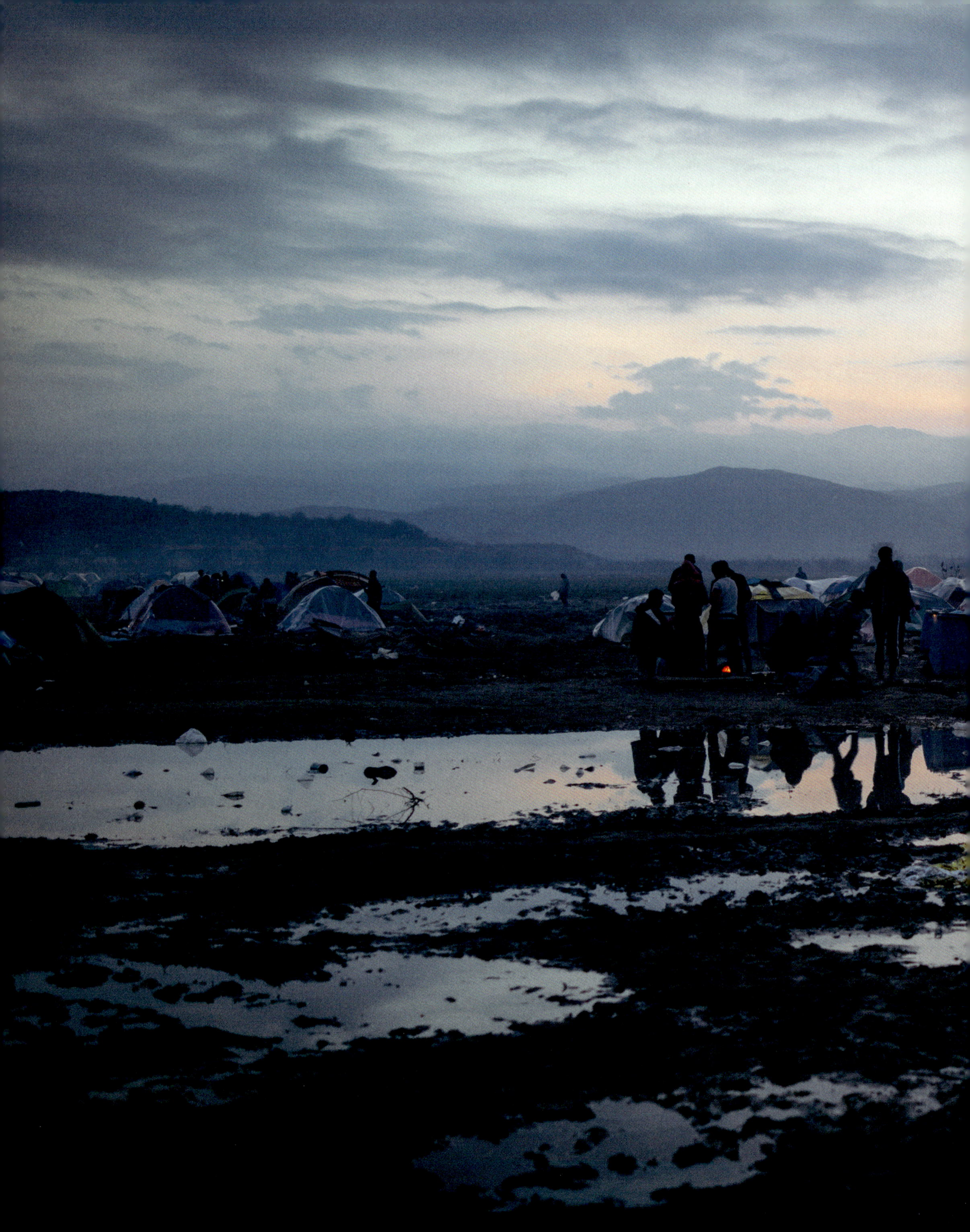

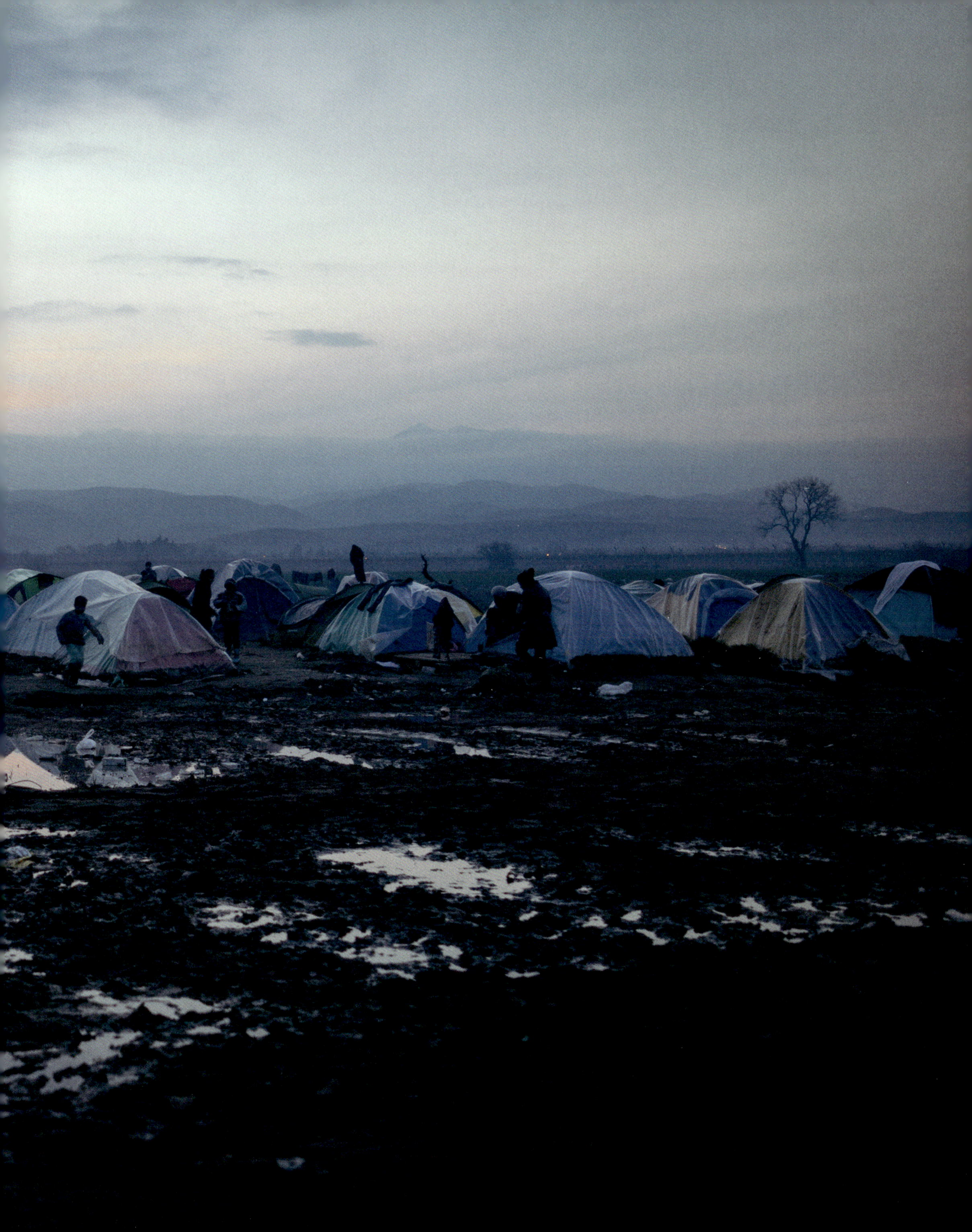

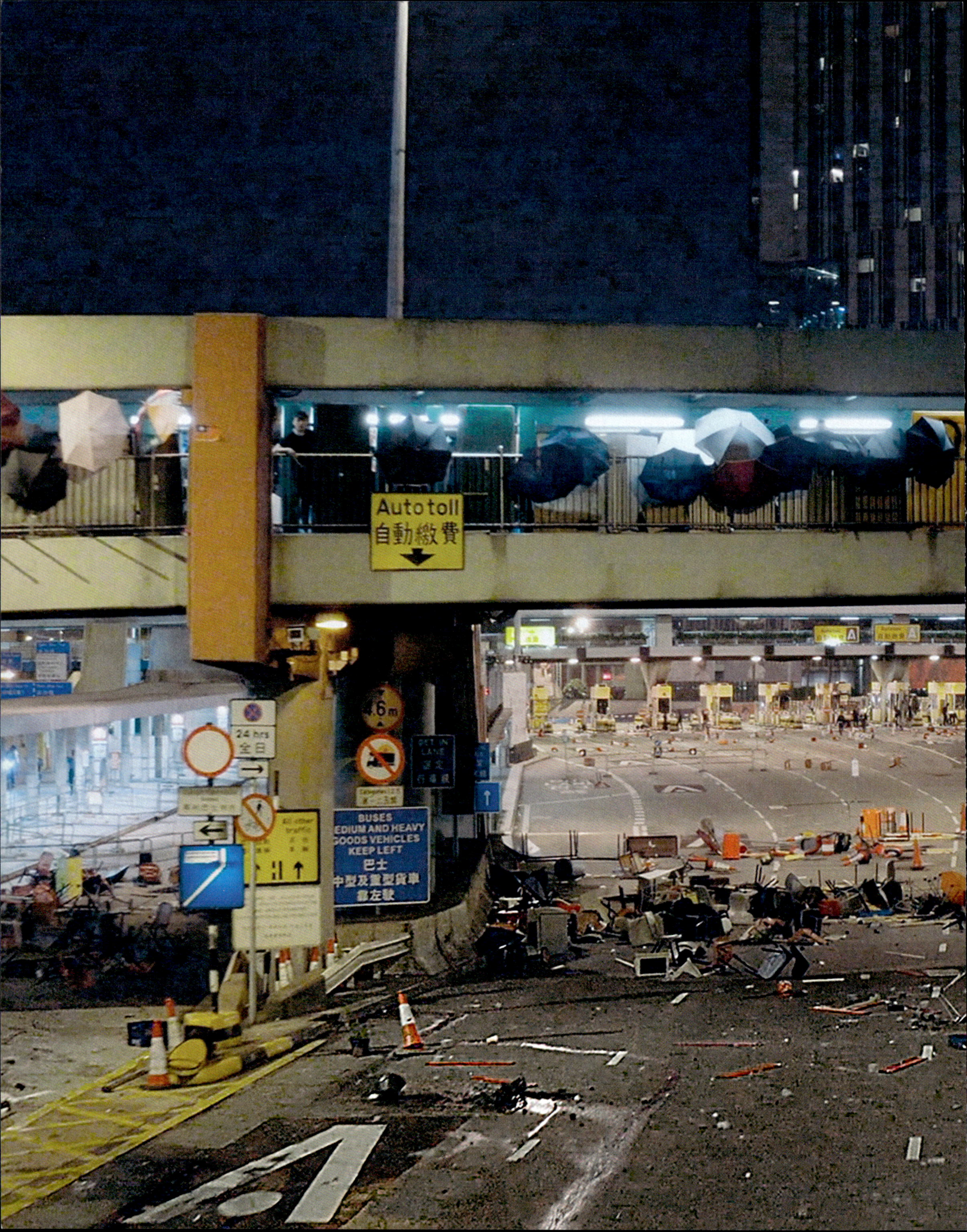
Auto toll
自動繳費
24 hrs
全日
BUSES
EDIUM AND HEAVY
GOODS VEHICLES
KEEP LEFT
巴士
中型及重型貨車
靠左駛

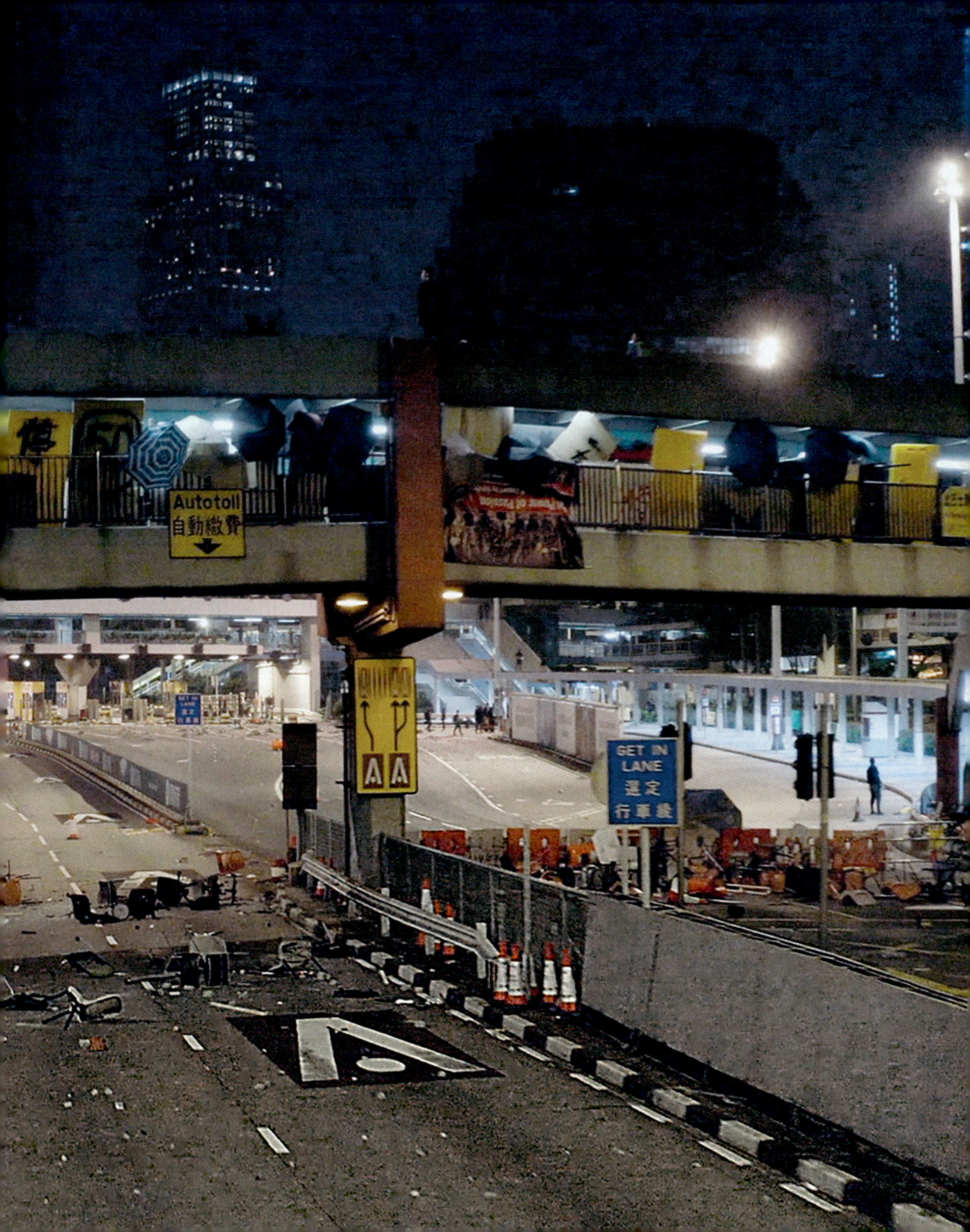
Autotoll
自動繳費
GET IN
LANE
選定
行車線

ON HUMAN RIGHTS

AI WEIWEI

At the core of human rights is the question of what it means to be human. To be human has specific implications: human self-awareness and the actions taken to uphold human dignity – these are what give the concept of humanity a special meaning.

Human self-awareness and human actions are embodied in the interplay between individual thought and language and the wider society, in economic security, the right to education, and the right to free association and free expression; it is human actions that create conditions for protecting expression and encouraging bold thinking. If we abandon efforts to uphold human dignity, we forfeit the essential meaning of being human, and when we waver in our commitment to the idea of human rights, we are abandoning our moral principles. What follow from such a failure are duplicity and folly, corruption and tyranny, and the endless stream of humanitarian crises that we see in the world today.

More than two centuries have passed since the concept of human rights was first proposed. During that time, humanity has gone through various stages of historical development and the world has seen enormous changes. In Europe, what was once a collection of colonialist, autocratic states has transformed into a democratic society with a capitalist orientation, establishing a democratic framework and a mechanism that protects individual rights. Under the new globalising order, other societies are also seeing structural changes, and the concept of human rights is facing grave challenges. In part the challenges stem from the disparate demands of countries in different stages of development, with contrasting economic situations and competing economic interests. But challenges also come from divergent conceptions of human rights, from divergent understandings of human dignity, morality and responsibility, and from different interpretations and applications of the core principles of human rights. In the contemporary world, as we weaken our grasp of the fundamental values and principles of human rights and humanitarianism, we risk losing our right, responsibility and power to uphold human dignity.

History shows that a moral failure is always accompanied by painful realities, visible everywhere. The global refugee crisis is worsening daily, and 70 million refugees have been forced to leave their homes by war and poverty. Our living environment is constantly being degraded, and the ecological balance is ever more fragile. Armed conflicts persist and potential political crises lurk; regional instabilities grow more acute; autocratic regimes brutally impose their will, while democratic government is in decline. Unreasoning and unrestrained expansion under a nationalist, capitalist order is exacerbating the global gap between rich and poor. Our views of the world have become more divided and more conflicted than ever before.

In many countries and many regions of the world, individuals have no chance to receive an education, no chance to access information or communicate freely, no chance to exercise their imagination and creativity and fulfil individual and social ideals, no chance to enjoy freedom of belief and freedom of association. Such rights and freedoms pose a fatal threat to autocracy and authoritarianism. This is why, in so many places, lawyers have been imprisoned, why journalists have been disappeared and murdered, why censorship has become so pervasive, why religious and non-governmental organisations have been ruthlessly suppressed. Today, corrupt regimes continue to benefit from reckless arms sales, and dictatorships enjoy the quiet support of capitalist nations. Religious divisions and regional disputes all feed into ongoing power plays. Their logic is simple: to weaken individual freedoms and strengthen the controls imposed by governments and dominant elites. The end result is that individuals are deprived of the right to live, denied freedom from fear and freedom of expression, or denied the right to maintain their living environment and their right to development.

The concept of human rights needs to be revised. Discussions of human rights used to focus on the one-dimensional relationship between state rights and individual rights, but now human rights involve a variety of multidimensional, mutually impacting relationships. Today, no matter whether demands are framed in terms of the rights of the individual or in terms of the goals pursued by political entities and interest groups, none of these agendas exist in isolation. Compared to other periods in history, the conditions governing human existence are now all the more globally interdependent.

The right of children to grow up and be educated, the right of women to receive protection, the right to conserve nature, the right to survival of other lives intimately connected with the survival of the human race – all these rights have now become major elements in the concept of human rights. As science and technology develop, authoritarian states invade privacy and limit personal freedom in the name of counter-terrorism and stability maintenance, intensifying psychological manipulation at all levels. Through controls of the Internet and command of facial recognition technology, authoritarian states tighten their grasp on people's thoughts and actions, threatening and even eliminating the political rights of groups that are seeking freedom. Similar kinds of controls are being imposed to varying degrees within the global context. From this we can see that under these new conditions, human rights have not gained a common understanding, and if discussion of human rights becomes narrow and shortsighted, it is bound to become nothing more than outdated, empty talk.

Today, Europe, the United States, Russia, China and other governments manufacture, possess and sell arms. If we fail to curb these dangerous practices that make armed conflict all the more likely, to pontificate about human rights is simply self-deluding. Likewise, if there are no limits placed on capitalist global expansion and the pervasive penetration of capital power, if there is no effort to curb the sustained assault by authoritarian governments on natural human impulses, a discussion of human rights is just idle chatter. Such a blatant abdication of responsibility can lead to no good outcome.

Human rights are shared values. When we talk about human rights, we are not talking about the rights of one individual or the rights of people in one part of the world – we are talking about the collective values of humanity. Human rights are our common possession, and shared human rights are all people's rights. When abuses are committed against anyone in any society, then all of us suffer injury and the dignity of humanity as a whole is compromised. By the same token, it is only when the rights of any individual and the rights of the people of any region receive our care and protection that humanity can achieve a shared redemption.

Such is the principle of human rights, in all its stark simplicity. But a shared understanding of that truth still eludes us. Why so? Could it be that we are too benighted, too selfish, too lacking in courage? Or, perhaps, it is rather because we are insincere, because we don't really love life enough: we con ourselves into imagining we can get away with not discharging our obligation to institute fairness and justice, we fool ourselves into thinking that chaos is acceptable, we are willing to entertain the idea that the world may well collapse in ruin, all hopes and dreams shattered.

Conversely, if we truly believe in the existence of values that we can all identify with and aspire to – a recognition of truth, an understanding of science, an appreciation of the self, a respect for life and a faith in society – then we need to eliminate obstacles to understanding, uphold the fundamental definition of humanity, affirm the shared value of human lives and other lives, and acknowledge the symbiotic interdependence of human beings and the environment. A belief in ourselves and a belief in others, a trust in humanitarianism's power to do good, and an earnest recognition of the value of life – these form the foundation for all human values and all human efforts.

TRANSLATED BY ALLAN H. BARR

Originally published in *Ai Weiwei: Bare Life*, ed. Sabine Eckmann, Mildred Lane Kemper Art Museum, Sam Fox School of Design and Visual Arts, Washington University in St Louis, St Louis MO, 2019

BIOGRAPHY

1957

Ai Weiwei is born in Beijing on 18 May 1957 to the writer and poet Ai Qing (1910–1996) and his wife, Gao Ying (b. 1934).

1958–75

During the first year of Ai Weiwei's life, his father, Ai Qing, is denounced as a rightist and exiled to Beidahuang, in Heilongjiang province, northeast China, together with his family. Eight years later, in 1966, they are transferred to Shihezi, in Xinjiang province, northwest China, where Ai Qing is forced to undergo further 'thought reform' through hard labour. This includes cleaning the village's communal toilets. The family returns to Beijing in 1975.

1978

Ai Weiwei enrols at the Beijing Film Academy and studies animation as part of the first class to admit students after the Cultural Revolution (1966–76).

1979

Ai Qing is rehabilitated and becomes a vice-chairman of the China Writers Association. Ai Weiwei is a founding member of the Stars art group, the first artist movement to react to and break away from the official aesthetic policies of the Chinese Communist Party.

1981–93

Ai Weiwei moves to the United States. Initially, he studies English in Pennsylvania and California and then relocates to New York in 1983, where he briefly studies at Parsons School of Design and the Art Students League. He makes a living from odd jobs, such as carpentry, babysitting, freelance photography and street portraiture.

1988

He has his first solo exhibition at Art Waves/Ethan Cohen in New York.

1993–96

Ai Weiwei returns to Beijing for the first time in 12 years to care for his ailing father. Ai begins collecting antique furniture and pottery. He also begins to edit and publish underground publications promoting the Chinese avant-garde. Ai Qing passes away on 5 May 1996.

1997

Together with Hans van Dijk (1946–2002) and Frank Uytterhaegen (1954–2011), Ai Weiwei establishes the China Art Archives and Warehouse in Beijing, the first independent contemporary art space in China.

1999

He designs and builds his studio house in Caochangdi, a village on the outskirts of northeast Beijing. He takes part in the 48th Venice Biennale, curated by Harald Szeemann (1933–2005).

2001

Ai Weiwei establishes Beijing Fake Cultural Development Ltd., his design and architectural practice. The name is a play on the English word 'fake' and its Chinese transliteration, which is a homonym for the English word 'fuck'.

2002–03

Ai Weiwei collaborates with the Swiss architects Herzog & de Meuron on the design of Beijing's National Stadium for the 2008 Summer Olympic Games.

2005

He begins a blog at the invitation of Chinese web portal Sina. His writings cover a wide range of issues, including social commentary, criticism of government policy, and his thoughts on art and architecture.

2007

Ai Weiwei presents *Fairytale* at *documenta 12*, bringing 1,001 Chinese citizens to Kassel, Germany.

2008–10

An earthquake in Sichuan province causes the deaths of about 90,000 people. Ai Weiwei launches a Citizens' Investigation to compile a name list of the more than 5,000 chidren who died when schools collapsed during the devastating quake. As a result, his blog is shut down permanently. He begins using Twitter and tweets at @aiww.

2008

Ai Weiwei criticises the Beijing Olympic Games and refuses to participate in the government's propaganda campaign. The Jiading district local government in Shanghai invites him to build a studio in Malu. Ai wins the Chinese Contemporary Art Award (CCAA) for his lifetime achievements in his work.

2009

The police raid Ai Weiwei's hotel room in Sichuan and detain him, preventing him from testifying on behalf of Tan Zuoren (b. 1954), a writer and activist investigating the shoddy construction of the schools that collapsed during the Sichuan earthquake and who stands accused of 'inciting subversion of state power'. Ai receives blows to the head during the incident and is later found to be suffering from a brain haemorrhage. He undergoes emergency surgery in Germany the following month.

2010

Ai Weiwei presents his large-scale installation *Sunflower Seeds* in the Tate Modern's Turbine Hall in London. The Shanghai government informs Ai that his newly built studio in Malu is an illegal construction and must be demolished.

2011

Ai Weiwei's Shanghai studio is demolished with less than 24 hours' notice. Chinese secret police arrest Ai at Beijing Capital International Airport and he is detained at a secret location for 81 days. He is released 'on bail, pending trial' without formal charges. His passport is confiscated and he is banned from travelling abroad.

2013

Ai Weiwei presents *S.A.C.R.E.D.* in the Church of Sant'Antonin during the 55th Venice Biennale.

2015

Amnesty International awards Ai Weiwei the Ambassador of Conscience Award for his work in defence of human rights. After his passport is returned, the artist relocates to Berlin to live and work there. He begins his Einstein Visiting Professorship at the University of the Arts in Berlin.

2016–17

Ai Weiwei visits the Greek isle of Lesbos. He witnesses at first hand the incoming refugee boats and meets those who have arrived at the Moria refugee camp. As director, producer and cinematographer, he creates *Human Flow*, a feature-length documentary on the global refugee condition. Ai and the film team visit more than 40 refugee camps across 23 countries and conduct over 600 interviews.

2018

In August, Ai Weiwei's studio in Beijing is demolished by the Chinese authorities without prior notice.

2021

He publishes his memoir, *1000 Years of Joys and Sorrows*. Ai Weiwei currently lives and works in various locations, including Beijing, Berlin, Cambridge (UK) and Lisbon.

AUTHOR BIOGRAPHIES

HAJNI ELIAS

Dr Hajni Elias was Senior Researcher at Sotheby's Chinese Works of Art department between 2001 and 2013. In 2018 she obtained her PhD from the University of Cambridge in the field of early Chinese cultural history. She is currently a Leverhulme Early Career Fellow at the Faculty of Asian and Middle Eastern Studies, University of Cambridge, where she teaches Chinese history, art and material culture. She is also a guest lecturer in the History of Art department at Cambridge. Her current research for the Leverhulme Trust explores artistic and cultural transmission among early societies in China and Southeast Asia along the Southwest Silk Road.

JAMES J. LALLY

James J. Lally is a Chinese art specialist and the founder of J. J. Lally & Co. in New York, a gallery presenting special exhibitions with scholarly catalogues of ancient Chinese ceramics, bronzes, jades, sculpture and other works of art from 1986 to 2020. Previously Lally was a director of Sotheby's. He participated in the establishment of Sotheby's auction sales in Hong Kong in 1973 and was named President of Sotheby's North America in 1985. Chinese works of art from J. J. Lally & Co. are now in museum collections including the British Museum, the Philadelphia Museum of Art, the Metropolitan Museum of Art, New York, the Museum of Fine Arts, Boston, the Tokyo Museum, the Shanghai Museum and many others.

JOHN TANCOCK

Born in London, John Tancock is a graduate of Downing College, Cambridge, and the Courtauld Institute of Art, London. After graduating he moved to the United States, where he started his career as a curator at the Philadelphia Museum of Art. In 1972 he moved to

Sotheby's in New York, where he became director of the newly established Contemporary Department before concentrating on European Impressionist and Modern paintings and sculpture. In recent years he has focused on contemporary Chinese art and was co-curator of the exhibition *DUCHAMP and/or/in CHINA* at the UCCA Center for Contemporary Art in Beijing in 2013, as well as *Ai Weiwei: Cubes and Trees* at Downing College, Cambridge, in 2016.

ELIZABETH BROWN

Elizabeth Brown is Curator, Contemporary Programmes (Temporary Cover) at Kettle's Yard, and is also a freelance curator with recent projects at Wysing Arts Centre in Cambridgeshire. Before joining Kettle's Yard, she was Assistant Curator at Wysing and was previously part of the exhibitions team at MK Gallery, Milton Keynes.

ANDREW NAIRNE

Andrew Nairne OBE has been Director of Kettle's Yard since 2011. He is a former director of Dundee Contemporary Arts and Modern Art Oxford. He has worked with numerous UK and international artists over three decades.

Published in 2022 by Kettle's Yard
on the occasion of the exhibition:

Ai Weiwei: The Liberty of Doubt
12 February – 19 June 2022

Kettle's Yard
University of Cambridge, Castle Street,
Cambridge CB3 0AQ, United Kingdom
kettlesyard.co.uk

Published in association with
and distribution by Ridinghouse

Ridinghouse
46 Lexington Street, London W1F 0LP
ridinghouse.co.uk

Distributed in the UK, Europe
and the rest of the world by ACC Art Books
Sandy Lane, Old Martlesham,
Woodbridge, Suffolk IP12 4SD
accartbooks.com

Distributed in the United States
and Canada by ARTBOOK | D.A.P.
75 Broad Street, Suite 630,
New York, NY 10004
artbook.com

British Library Cataloguing-in-Publication
Data. A full catalogue record of this book is
available from the British Library.

ISBN 978-1-909932-72-2

Edited by Elizabeth Brown and Andrew Nairne

Ridinghouse Publisher: Sophie Kullmann
Ridinghouse Senior Editor: Aimee Selby
Design: A Practice for Everyday Life
Production: A Practice for Everyday Life
and Sophie Kullmann
Printed in Italy by Verona Libri

PHOTO CREDITS

All images, with the exception of those stated
below, are courtesy Ai Weiwei Studio

pp.57–69, 74, 78, 83: Tip Photography
pp.33–48, 70–71: Jo Underhill

Cover: A Chinese lacquered greystone
fragmentary hand, clutching a bottle,
stone, in Northern Qi dynasty style
Image: Tip Photography

Back cover: Ai Weiwei, *Marble Takeout Box*, 2015
Image: Courtesy Ai Weiwei Studio

Back cover (inside flap): Ai Weiwei,
Surveillance Camera with Plinth, 2014
Image: Courtesy Ai Weiwei Studio

Inside cover (front): Thierry Bal,
Portrait of Ai Weiwei, 2021
Image: Courtesy of Thierry Bal

Ai Weiwei: The Liberty of Doubt
Kettle's Yard

Chair: Bridget Kendall MBE
Director: Andrew Nairne OBE
Assistant Director: Susie Biller

Exhibition devised by Ai Weiwei
Curated by Elizabeth Brown,
Guy Haywood and Andrew Nairne

Technical management: Tom Noblett
with Steve Penney

Exhibition realised with support
of Ai Weiwei Studio and Lisson Gallery

All loans to the exhibition courtesy
Ai Weiwei Studio

AI WEIWEI AT KETTLE'S YARD
EXHIBITION CIRCLE

We are grateful for the support of the following:

LISSON GALLERY

Charles and Angela Chadwyck-Healey, John
and Jennifer Crompton, Sabine Jaccaud, Suling
Chan Mead, The Porthmeor Fund, Marc and
Rachel Polonsky, Samantha de Reus and Felix
Zhang, Bianca and Stuart Roden, Giles and
Sonia Coode-Adams, Dr Carol Atack and Alex
van Someren, The Andrew and Fiona Blake
Trust Fund, Eve Corder, Dr Claire and Professor
Martin Daunton, The Hubbard Family, Midge
and Simon Palley, Jonathan and Nicole Scott,
Nicci Steele-Williams, Alex Haidas, Professor
Keith Moffat, and all those who wish to
remain anonymous

KETTLE'S YARD STAFF

Imogen Alexander, Susie Biller, Nastasha Boyce,
Renata Bralska, Elizabeth Brown, Dawn Bulmer,
Deborah Carnwath, Janet Carrington, Lauren
Clemmet, Christine Cowling-Jones, Chris Deane,
Helen Dickman, Miriam Goddard, Yasemin Gyford,
Beth Hague, Francis Hardy, Guy Haywood,
Lucinda Hooi, My Linh Le, Antonia Leslie,
Rebecca Lindum Greene, Andrew Maddocks,
Sreenandini Marikinti, Katie Maynard, Shirley-
Anne McAndrew, Alison McTaggart, Adéla
Minaříková, Andrew Nairne, Phil Neale, Alison
Newbery, Tom Noblett, Aaron Ossia, Steve
Penney, Elena-Doina Pop, Freya Pryce, Laura
Pryke, Habda Rashid, Sabrina Rippon, Daniela
Riva Rossi, Karina Sawyer, Vincenzo Sgaramella,
Elizabeth Singleton, Eliza Spindel, Andrew
Smith, Karen Thomas, Amy Tobin, Kim Watson,
Kathryn Westmore, Ellie Williams

With thanks to our team of freelance technicians

SUPPORT AT KETTLE'S YARD

Kettle's Yard relies on the generosity of
supporters to care for the collection and historic
buildings, and enable us to offer a full programme
of activities, from exhibitions, learning activities
and music to publications and research. All gifts,
large and small, help to safeguard the collection
for future generations and enable others to
enjoy Kettle's Yard now and in the future.

There are a variety of ways in which you can
help support Kettle's Yard and also benefit as
a UK or US taxpayer. For more information
please visit kettlesyard.co.uk/supporters.

DIRECTOR'S CIRCLE

Dr Carol Atack and Alex van Someren, Lily
Bacon and Dr Andy Harter, Sir Charles and
Lady Chadwyck-Healey, John and Jennifer
Crompton, Samantha de Reus and Felix Zhang
and those who wish to remain anonymous

EDE CIRCLE

Michael Allen OBE and Marjolein Wytzes,
Stuart Ansell, Helaine and Yorick Blumenfeld,
Dr Sophie Bowness, Dr David and Mrs Rosalind
Cleevely, Jennifer Crouch, Dr Claire and
Professor Martin Daunton, Peter Gerrard, Dr
Sean Gorvy and the late Gael Gorvy Robertson,
Jenny Little, Tim Llewellyn OBE, Nicki and
Christie Marrian, Suling Chan Mead, Professor
Keith Moffat, Jonathan and Nicole Scott, Toby
Smeeton and Anya Waddington, Professor
Elizabeth Simpson OBE, Alan Swerdlow and
Jeremy Greenwood, Stuart Wilkinson and
those who wish to remain anonymous

THE FRIENDS OF KETTLE'S YARD

CORPORATE SUPPORTERS

Cheffins, EY, Eve Waldron Design, Tayabali &
White, Langham Press, Anna's Flower Farm,
A Practice for Everyday Life

Kettle's Yard is grateful to the following for
their support: Arts Council England, Cambridge
City Council, Cambridge County Council,
Clore Duffield Foundation, The Esmée Fairbairn
Foundation, Hinrichsen Foundation, The Ragdoll
Foundation, Research England, RVW Trust

ARTIST ACKNOWLEDGEMENTS

Ai Weiwei Studio Team: Yun-hua Chen, Cui Xing,
Camilla Eggert, Gui Nuo, Monira Kleineidam, Li
Dongxu, Meiling Lin, Ma Yan, Jennifer Ng, Nuno
Rodrigues, Annette Schryen, Nadine Stenke,
Sun Mo, Kimberly Sung, Wang Fen, Xia Xing,
Xu Ye, Chin-Chin Yap

With special thanks to the following: Susan
Lintott, Chris Mao, Lisson Gallery, Greg Hilty,
Courtney Plummer, John Tancock, James J.
Lally, Dr Hajni Elias, Ai Lao

KETTLE'S YARD Ridinghouse UNIVERSITY OF CAMBRIDGE MUSEUMS & BOTANIC GARDEN Research England

The stamps bear the Chinese characters 贋齋, ‘Fake Studio’